Acknowledgements

I should like to thank the many people who helped in this enquiry, not least the informants for the time and thought they gave to the interviews.

For their advice and comments at the various stages of the enquiry, and for their co-operation in ensuring the smooth running of the study I am particularly grateful to the staff of the courts in the Greater London area, to members of H M Prison Service, and to members of the James Committee.

Finally, this report is the result of the work of many people and I should like to thank other members of the research staff and the staff of the Technical Branches of Social Survey Division—Sampling, Field, Primary Analysis and Computing—for their valuable contributions.

OFFICE OF POPULATION CENSUSES AND SURVEYS
SOCIAL SURVEY DIVISION

Crown Court or magistrates' court?

An enquiry carried out at the request of the Home Office on behalf of the James Committee which was set up to review the distribution of criminal business between the Crown Court and magistrates' courts.

An examination of the factors affecting the venue decisions made by a sample of defendants in criminal cases heard at courts in the Greater London area.

Janet Gregory

London : Her Majesty's Stationery Office

ISBN 0 11 700814 1*

Contents

List of tables

1 Introduction

In September 1973 the then Home Secretary and the Lord Chancellor appointed a Committee, headed by Lord Justice James, with the following terms of reference:

> 'to consider within the framework of the existing court structure what should be the distribution of business between the Crown Court and the magistrates' courts; and what changes in law and practice are desirable to that end.'

1.1 Background

Despite considerable increases since 1970 in the number of courtrooms and judges, during the first quarter of 1973, in London, the average waiting period experienced by a defendant between committal for trial to the Crown Court and the trial itself was 13 weeks for those in custody, and just over 24 weeks for those released on bail. Outside London this period was kept to about eight weeks.

The Interdepartmental Committee on the Business of the Criminal Courts, reporting in 1961, had recommended that, '. . . it should be the aim of all types of court to keep the waiting period (that is, the period between committal for trial and the trial) in every case as short as possible, and those concerned should not be content merely to secure that the trial takes place within eight weeks.'[1]

This Committee set out five main reasons why it felt the delay should be kept to a minimum; these apply equally today.

(a) Where an offence has been committed which has given rise to concern or anxiety, either at a local or national level, it is in the public's interest that there should be no delay in deciding upon the innocence or guilt of the accused person and, if necessary, in fixing the penalty.

(b) The period before trial is an anxious one for the accused and should not be protracted.

(c) The delay in bringing a case to court may cause real distress to some witnesses who dread the thought of appearing at court and giving formal evidence.

(d) Evidence may go stale over a long period; the recollections of the witnesses may not be so fresh in their minds.

(e) Persons held on remand, awaiting trial, must put a strain on the resources of an already overpopulated prison system.

1.2 Current practice

Currently, offences are broadly classified into two groups, 'indictable offences' and 'summary offences'. Generally speaking, indictable offences are those which are thought to be so serious or complex that they must be tried before a judge at the Crown Court, and summary offences are those of a less serious nature which are normally dealt with by magistrates. However, for some indictable offences the defendant may be tried by magistrates if he consents, and similarly there are some summary offences where the defendant may claim trial at the Crown Court, before a judge and jury. This is an oversimplification of the situation and the complexities of the classification of offences, and the conditions under which an option for the place of trial is possible are explained more fully in Appendix A.

---

[1] *Report of the Interdepartmental Committee on the Business of the Criminal Courts* Cmnd 1289 Home Office 1961 para 32 p 10.

The increasing delays that defendants are experiencing in coming to trial are due to the considerable increases in the volume of work that is being dealt with by the Crown Court. This in turn is partly due to the increases in crime and crime detection, but can also be attributed to more cases being passed up to the Crown Court from the magistrates' courts.

Table 1 shows the numbers of persons committed for trial to a higher court for indictable offences and for non-indictable offences for the years from 1966 to 1973, and the proportions of the total numbers of persons proceeded against for indictable offences and non-indictable offences that these represent.

It can be calculated that over this period there has been an increase of just over one-third in the total numbers of persons proceeded against, with proceedings for indictable offences increasing at a slightly higher rate than proceedings for non-indictable offences. Thus the total business of the courts is increasing.

Table 1 *Numbers of persons of all ages proceeded against for indictable and non-indictable offences 1966–73 in England and Wales*[1]

Year	Indictable offences			Non-indictable offences		
	Total persons proceeded against	of whom committed for trial	Percentage committed for trial	Total persons proceeded against	of whom committed for trial	Percentage committed for trial
1966	250,211	26,473	10·6	1,269,270	5,719	0·5
1967	261,169	27,673	10·6	1,402,708	6,014	0·4
1968	277,718	30,176	10·9	1,387,724	5,915	0·4
1969	329,702	37,246	11·3	1,372,584	6,121	0·4
1970	350,705	42,852	12·2	1,426,059	7,589	0·5
1971	350,872	44,822	12·8	1,444,872	8,944	0·6
1972	373,338	48,942	13·1	1,569,162	9,646	0·6
1973	365,505	48,333	13·2	1,673,554	11,375	0·7

The table shows that for non-indictable offences in each year, less than 1 per cent of persons were committed for trial to a higher court, but it can be seen that the actual numbers of persons being sent to a higher court for trial for non-indictable offences has almost doubled between 1966 and 1973. For indictable offences, the proportions of persons committed to trial to a higher court is much higher and has risen from 10·6 per cent in 1966 to 13·2 per cent in 1973 representing an 83 per cent increase in the actual number of persons committed over this period. If then both indictable and non-indictable offences are considered, it can be estimated that between 1966 and 1973 the percentage increase in persons being committed for trial to the Crown Court has risen to 85 per cent while the corresponding increase in the business of the magistrates' courts is only 33 per cent. It has been estimated that if present trends continue then by 1982 the Crown Court will need to deal with about 70,000 *cases*.

Clearly one way of relieving the current and future pressures on the Crown Court would be to have a greater proportion of cases dealt with at magistrates' courts.

1.3 The James Committee

One of the tasks of the James Committee was to review the existing criteria which determine whether a case is dealt with by a judge and jury at the Crown Court, or whether it can be tried by magistrates. The Committee invited both organisations and individuals to submit evidence expressing views on the present system, which in a considerable proportion of cases allows the defendant to choose the venue for his trial, and to suggest new procedures for determining whether a case is dealt with by a magistrates' court or by a judge and jury in the Crown Court.

The James Committee felt that in addition to receiving evidence and opinions from persons and organisations with professional interest in law and criminology, they

---

[1]*Criminal Statistics: England and Wales Home Office* HMSO.

should also know why, under the existing legal system, some defendants when given the right to choose where they want to have their case heard, opt to stay at the magistrates' court, while others choose to go for trial at the Crown Court before a judge and jury.

It was felt that this information would be forthcoming if a survey were to be conducted with the aim of finding out from defendants, who had recently had their cases disposed of, the reasons they had chosen to go for trial at the Crown Court, or had elected summary trial at a magistrates' court, and their attitudes and their satisfaction with their trial and sentence. The survey would also attempt to find out how defendants felt about some of the changes that might be made on the recommendation of the James Committee.

The Social Survey Division of the Office of Population Censuses and Surveys was asked by the Home Office to carry out this survey for the James Committee.

Preliminary discussions with the Home Office and a sub-committee of the James Committee to discuss the feasibility of a survey took place in February 1974. The James Committee needed to have the results of the survey by November 1974, and to meet this fieldwork had to be carried out mid–April to mid–May. This was an exceedingly tight timetable which very much affected what could be done.

1.4 The survey design

The timetable and the resources available meant that at most about 800 interviews could be attempted: a decision had then to be made as to which groups of defendants should be interviewed. It was decided that Social Survey resources would best be used by limiting the enquiry to those people who might have had some direct experience of making a choice themselves as to where their cases would be heard. The timetable and resources available also meant that the enquiry had to be restricted to one area, and it was decided that the resources would best be used by conducting the survey in Greater London, where the delay to defendants in getting to court is greatest.

Domestic and civil proceedings were excluded from the enquiry as these did not come within the terms of reference of the James Committee. Juvenile offenders were also excluded since it is not generally possible for defendants who are under 17 to choose the venue for their trial themselves. Appeal cases were also excluded because no choice of venue is involved.

The three samples selected for interview from court records were therefore restricted to defendants whose cases included at least one criminal offence of the type that carries an option of venue for trial; that is the case had to include either an indictable offence which could be tried summarily by magistrates, or a summary offence which could be tried on indictment at the Crown Court before a judge and jury, or it had to include a hybrid offence. Thus defendants whose offences were so serious as to be tried only on indictment at the Crown Court, or were of the type that could be tried summarily only at a magistrates' court, were excluded.

Although the samples were restricted to defendants whose cases included at least one offence that carried an option of venue for trial, it would not have always been the defendant who determined where the case would be heard. In certain circumstances the venue for trial would have been determined either by the prosecution or by the magistrate(s). For example, a defendant charged with a hybrid offence which carries a maximum sentence of less than three months' imprisonment on summary conviction at a magistrates' court has no right to choose trial on indictment at the Crown Court. For other types of offences the situation is less clear: defendants charged with indictable offences which may be tried summarily by magistrates only have the option of choosing the venue for their trial themselves if the court considers that the case is not serious enough to justify trial on indictment at the Crown Court. If the prosecution recommends a Crown Court hearing, usually because the circumstances of the offence are regarded as serious, then committal proceedings are begun and the defendant is not usually given the option of staying and being tried before magistrates.

When selecting the samples it was not possible to find out whether the defendant had chosen the venue for trial himself: this had to be determined during the interview, and defendants who reported having had no choice of venue were dealt with separately in the questionnaire.

It was estimated that about 800 interviews could be attempted. Since the intention was to compare the views of defendants who had been tried at magistrates' courts with those of defendants who had been tried at the Crown Court, approximately equal numbers of these two groups of defendants were needed for interview. However it was known that proportionately many more defendants choose to be tried at a magistrates' court than choose to go for trial at the Crown Court. Also, because of the way records are kept at the courts, the two groups of defendants had to be selected independently from magistrates' courts and from various Crown Court centres, and so in order to obtain approximately equal numbers of the two groups they were sampled differentially from the records at the two levels of court. Defendants whose cases had been tried and disposed of at magistrates' courts were selected over a three-day period from records held at a random selection of half the magistrates' courts in the Greater London area, while defendants appearing for trial at the Crown Court were selected over a ten-day period from all the Crown Court centres in Greater London dealing with criminal business.

As a result of this sampling procedure, the sample of defendants selected from magistrates' courts cannot be added to the sample of defendants selected from the Crown Court centres without some reweighting. It is estimated that a factor of about x7 should be applied to the sample of defendants whose cases were tried and disposed of at magistrates' courts in order that it corresponds to the sample of defendants whose cases were tried and disposed of at the Crown Court and who were selected from Crown Court records.

During preliminary discussions about the survey it became apparent that a third sample would be required: this would comprise defendants whose cases had been tried before magistrates, who had been convicted by them, but who then had been committed to the Crown Court for sentence. Although such defendants would have chosen to be tried by magistrates, it was thought that their views on their trial might differ from those of defendants who had been tried and had their cases disposed of by magistrates, and that their views on their sentence might differ from those of defendants whose entire case had been dealt with by Crown Court judges.

Since the samples were to include only those defendants whose cases had been completed, defendants tried at a magistrates' court and sentenced at the Crown Court were selected from records held at the Crown Court centres. The method of selecting the sample had the advantage of producing a rather larger number of this third group of defendants than would have been obtained from magistrates' courts' records and constituted an adequate third sample group. Full details of the sample selection are given in Appendix B.

1.5 The interview sample

A total of 792 defendants were selected for interview. Interviewing took place from mid–April to mid–May 1974, and 544 full interviews were returned. Full details of response rates and an analysis of non-response are given in Appendix B and are summarised in Table 2.

Table 2 *Summary of response for each of the three sample groups*

	Venue for trial					
	Disposal at					
	Crown Court		Magistrates' court		Crown Court	
	Nos	%	Nos	%	Nos	%
Interviews achieved	262	71	225	66	57	73
Interviews refused	18	5	32	9	3	4
Other non-contacts	91	24	86	25	13	23
Interviews attempted: base	371	100	343	100	73	100

While the response rates were lower than we would have liked, two of the sample groups included foreigners who had returned home and all three included defendants who had given 'accommodation' or 'convenience' addresses.

A comparison of non-respondents and respondents in the three samples showed no marked differences in any of the three samples between those co-operating in the enquiry and those whom we were unable to interview. Any conclusions drawn are therefore unlikely to be affected by the level of non-response.

1.6 The interview questionnaires

Three separate questionnaires were developed for use in this enquiry; one for those defendants whose cases had been tried and disposed of at magistrates' courts, one for defendants who had gone for trial to the Crown Court, and the third for those defendants who had been committed to the Crown Court from the magistrates' court for sentence. These three questionnaires in conjunction with the information originally returned from the courts on the sampling forms provided the basis for the results of this study.

The timetable imposed on the enquiry did not allow a pilot study to be carried out; this would have assisted in the development of a final questionnaire. The three questionnaires were therefore designed on the basis of information and knowledge gained from visits to both types of court and from discussions with court staff.

Each of the three questionnaires covered seven main areas which related both to an individual's own trial and to court procedure in general.

1.6.1 *Areas of enquiry:*

(a) previous experience of both levels of court either as a defendant or in some other capacity;

(b) knowledge of the differences between the two levels of court: sentencing powers, procedure, court personnel;

(c) reasons for the choice made: including advice from other people, the role of solicitors, and the contribution made by the police;

(d) satisfaction with the trial and the outcome; a defendant's own assessment of what might have happened had the choice of venue been different;

(e) dissatisfaction with any aspect of the trial or its outcome;

(f) defendants' suggestions of areas for improvement in court procedure;

(g) the importance on this occasion of being able to determine the venue for trial and its importance for a range of other offences.

It was known that some defendants would never have been given the option of choosing where their case would be heard because of the nature or the circumstances of their offence, and also it was anticipated that some defendants would be unaware that they had determined the venue for their trial themselves. However when the samples of defendants were selected from court records it had not been possible to determine who had made the decision regarding venue for trial, and as it would have been inappropriate to ask for a defendant's reasons for making the choice he did when the option had never been put to him or when he denied being given the choice, this had to be discovered during the interview.

Defendants were therefore asked whether they personally had said where they wanted their case to be heard, or whether they had no say in the matter. Those who said they played no part in the decision were reminded of the procedure at the magistrates' court and then asked if they remembered the clerk of the court asking whether they wanted their case heard before magistrates or before a judge and jury. Those defendants who maintained that they did not remember the option being put to them were then recorded as having had no personal choice of venue for their trial, and the subsequent questions put to them were modified accordingly.

Chapter 2 looks at those defendants who reported having no personal option as to where their case was heard, and attempts to distinguish between those who were given no choice of venue, and those who, despite having made the choice, were unaware of doing so.

1.7 Conducting the interview

On this particular study, the people who were selected for interview and the information about them which had been recorded from court documents presented special problems for interviewers.

Normally Social Survey interviewers give a full explanation of the purpose of the survey they are working on only when they have contacted the person they wish to interview, they then go on to explain for whom the survey is being conducted, the way the sample was selected, its random nature, the voluntary aspect of co-operation and the confidentiality of the information collected.

On this study it was particularly important that both the purpose of the survey and the nature of the sample should be explained only to the sampled defendant, and not to other members of the household who might be unaware of the informant's court appearance.

A number of defendants selected for interview were resident in penal institutions and this again involved taking special precautions to ensure the confidentiality of information given during the interview. All the interviewing at penal institutions was carried out in private; separate rooms, usually those used for consultations with solicitors, were set aside by the prison staff for interviewers and their informants; no third person was present. Co-operation was of course voluntary, and only one refusal was obtained from the 'in-custody' groups.

Informants were sometimes initially difficult to convince that the circumstances of their offence would not be discussed. However, once the interview was under way any antagonism on the part of the informant to the subject matter of the enquiry quickly disappeared, and there was generally a high level of interest in the questions themselves and in the purpose and aims of the survey. The interview took an average of 45 minutes.

2 Was a choice of venue for trial offered to the defendant?

Before defendants could be asked to explain why they had exercised their option of venue for trial in a particular way, those defendants who denied having been given any personal choice had to be identified.

Table 3 shows the number of defendants in each of three samples who reported having had no personal choice of venue for their trial, and the proportions of the total number of interviews they represent.[1]

Table 3 *Numbers and percentages of defendants in each of the three samples who were recorded as having had no personal choice of venue for their trial*

	Venue for trial					
	Crown Court		Magistrates' court			
	Disposal at					
	Crown Court		Magistrates' court		Crown Court	
	Nos	%	Nos	%	Nos	%
Defendant chose venue	166	63	203	90	43	75
Defendants who did not choose venue for trial themselves	96	37	22	10	14	25
Total number interviewed: base	262	100	225	100	57	100

The questionnaires returned for all defendants recorded as having had no personal choice of venue were scrutinised to see if it was possible to distinguish between cases where the defendant would not have been given a choice of venue, because of the nature or circumstances of his offence, and those where it seemed likely that the defendant had failed to appreciate that the option had, in fact, been given and the venue for trial was the result of his own choosing.

2.1 Probable reasons for not exercising the option of venue for trial

2.1.1 *Those defendants whose cases were heard and disposed of at magistrates' courts: 22 defendants*

Five defendants were charged with hybrid offences which carried no right on the part of the defendant to choose trial on indictment at the Crown Court. Therefore these defendants were correct in reporting that they had been given no choice of venue for their trial.

The nature of the offences charged against the remaining 17 defendants meant that they must have chosen to stay and be tried before magistrates and hence failed to

---

[1] It should be remembered that not all defendants who are tried summarily by magistrates can be sure that their cases will be finally disposed of at the magistrates' court. In certain circumstances they may be committed for sentence to the Crown Court. The fact that the venue for trial and the venue for disposal of a case may be different is shown in the headings to tables throughout the report.

appreciate that their summary trial at the magistrates' court had been the result of their own choosing.

Eight defendants were legally represented at the magistrates' court; for these defendants the solicitor may have been responsible for the venue decision. These eight included one defendant who said he could not hear what the clerk of the court had been saying, and one who had been on drugs at the time of his appearance, and reported having very little idea of what had been going on.

One defendant spontaneously reported being unable to 'hear what the man at the front (the clerk) was on about'.

For the remaining nine defendants there is no readily available explanation, other than the suggestion that the concept of making a personal choice might be less easily identified by this entire group than by those who chose trial at the Crown Court. These defendants were tried at a magistrates' court as a result of not exercising their option to go to the Crown Court, and what took place as a result may not have been regarded as the outcome of a personal choice—summary trial at a magistrates' court took place 'by default'.

2.1.2 *Those defendants whose cases were tried at magistrates' courts, but who were committed by the magistrates to the Crown Court for sentence: 14 defendants*

Only one defendant from this group had legal representation at the magistrates' court and the venue decision might therefore have been made without his knowledge.

It would appear that no defendant was committed for sentence to the Crown Court as an 'incorrigible rogue'.

The remaining 13 defendants therefore must have failed to appreciate that they themselves had determined the venue for their trial, either because they had not understood the procedure at court, or because they did not regard agreeing to summary trial at a magistrates' court as exercising a choice.

2.1.3 *Those defendants whose cases were tried and disposed of at the Crown Court: 96 defendants*

Four defendants were charged with hybrid offences which did not carry the right on the part of the defendant to choose trial on indictment at the Crown Court. The venue for their trial would have been determined by the court on the application of the prosecution. Seventeen defendants were charged with hybrid offences which allowed the defendant to choose trial by judge and jury if the prosecution initially requested summary trial at a magistrates' court. Of these 17, 10 defendants spontaneously mentioned that the prosecution had asked for their case to go to the Crown Court, and hence these 10 defendants correctly reported having no option of venue for trial. There was no such corroborating evidence for the remaining seven defendants in this group.

However 14 defendants charged with indictable offences which could have been tried by magistrates with their consent offered the information that the prosecution had said that because of the seriousness of their offences they would have to be dealt with at the Crown Court.

A further 14 defendants charged with the same category of offence reported that because a co-defendant had chosen to go to the Crown Court, they had been given no choice of venue themselves and had been obliged to go to the Crown Court with their co-defendant(s). Although legal practice does not require co-defendants to be tried at the same court, it is normal practice for co-defendants to be dealt with together. It is therefore probable that these 14 defendants were dealt with in the way they reported.

Burglary:

The offence of burglary is covered by legislation acknowledged to be confusing. For some offences of burglary, for example where force is involved, the offences may be tried only on indictment at the Crown Court while for other types of burglary the offence may either be dealt with on indictment at the Crown Court or summarily at a magistrates' court, with the consent of the accused. However the different types of burglary and the appropriate procedures for dealing with them are not categorised separately under different sections of the Theft Act. In recording details of the offence from court records it was not possible to distinguish between 'indictable burglary' and offences of burglary which could be dealt with either summarily by magistrates or by trial on indictment at the Crown Court.

Twenty-nine defendants recorded as charged with burglary reported having had no personal choice of venue for their trial. Two of these said that because they used force they had to 'go up': if the use of force was included in the original charge then they would indeed have had no option and these two cases should never have been included in the sample drawn from records for interview. Twelve defendants charged with burglary reported that the police, the bench, or their solicitor had told them that there would be no choice of where their case was to be heard: we would accept this, but it is not clear whether there was no effective choice because the charge was 'indictable burglary' or whether there was no choice because the prosecution had requested trial at the Crown Court. For the remaining 14 defendants charged with burglary there was no evidence to support their claim that they were never given a choice of venue.

Conspiracy:

Three defendants (in apparently unrelated cases) reported being charged with conspiracy: correctly they said this meant they had to go to the Crown Court for trial. However they added that once they had been committed for trial the conspiracy charges were dropped. The documents used in drawing the sample from Crown Court records showed no mention of conspiracy charges and as such these three cases had been included as eligible for interview.

The remaining 15 defendants tried on indictment at the Crown Court and reporting no personal choice of venue for their trial were all charged with various categories of offence which would have required their consent to summary trial at a magistrates' court. These defendants therefore were either sent to the Crown Court following a request for trial at the higher court by the prosecution, or following a request for summary trial at the magistrates' court by the prosecution, the defendant must have chosen to go before a judge and jury and yet not appreciated that he had made the decision himself.

2.2 Summary

Table 4 shows the probable reasons for defendants reporting having had no option as to where their case should be heard.

It can be seen from this table that the proportions of defendants in the three samples for whom there was no explanation as to why they would not have been given an option of venue for their trial are appreciable.

It has already been stated that some defendants who were tried at magistrates' courts will probably have failed to appreciate that they made a personal choice of venue. Lack of comprehension on the part of the defendant therefore probably accounts for 8 per cent of the group disposed of at magistrates' courts and 25 per cent of those tried at magistrates' courts but committed for sentence, for whom there is no other available explanation. However, it is thought unlikely that any sizeable proportion of the group who were tried at the Crown Court will have failed to appreciate that they were responsible for the venue of their trial. Choosing trial on indictment at the Crown Court is a positive act involving rejecting trial at a magistrates' court where one is already appearing, and opting to go elsewhere, contrary to the request of the prosecution. A decision to leave the magistrates' court and wait for an appearance at a higher level of court is unlikely to be forgotten or made unwittingly. This is not to say that the implications of the choice will always have been understood. It is suggested therefore that the majority of defendants, for whom there is no explanation either from the completed questionnaire or from the sampling data forms as to why they had no personal choice of venue, had in fact been sent to the Crown Court at the request of the prosecution.

Had the timetable for this survey permitted a pilot study to be conducted these particular problems might have become apparent, and it might have been possible at the sampling stage to have obtained further information about defendants who were being sampled from Crown Court records, from the records of their cases held at magistrates'

Table 4 *Numbers and percentages of defendants in each of the three samples who reported having had no option of venue for their trial, and probable reasons why the choice was not given to the defendant*

	Crown Court		Magistrates' court			
	Disposal at					
	Crown Court		Magistrates' court		Crown Court	
	Nos	%	Nos	%	Nos	%
Total number of defendants interviewed	262	100	225	100	57	100
Defendant reported exercising option	166	63	203	90	43	75
Defendant reported having had no option	96	37	22	10	14	25
Probable reason for having had no option						
Offence(s) did not carry option included in error	5	2	—	—	—	—
Offences carried option:						
(a) for prosecution only	4	1	5	2	—	—
(b) prosecution chose venue: defendant therefore had no choice	36	14	—	—	—	—
(c) co-defendant chose venue	14	6	—	—	—	—
No explanation	37	14	17	8	14	25

courts. Bearing in mind the shortcomings of the information at our disposal, we would nevertheless estimate that probably between 8 per cent and 25 per cent of defendants who were actually responsible for determining the venue for their trial themselves, failed to appreciate the part they had played.

Clearly those defendants who denied having exercised a personal choice in the venue for their trial could not be asked why they had preferred one level of court to another.[1] The following section which discusses a defendant's own reasons for choosing trial on indictment at the Crown Court or summary trial at a magistrates' court therefore refers only to those three groups of defendants who acknowledged being personally responsible for the venue of their trial.

---

[1] Table C1 p 76 shows the venue for trial that these defendants would have chosen had they been given the option.

3 Defendants who reported choosing the venue for their trial

Of the 262 defendants who had been tried at the Crown Court, 166, 63 per cent, reported that the venue for their trial had been their own choice. Of the 225 defendants whose cases had been tried and disposed of by magistrates, 203, 90 per cent, reported choosing the venue for their trial themselves and of the 57 defendants whose cases were tried by magistrates, but who were sentenced by a Crown Court judge, 43, 75 per cent, reported that the venue for their trial had been their own choice.

Chapter 2 looked at the defendants in each of the three sample groups who reported having been given no choice of where they wanted their case heard, and attempted to explain why this might have been so. If however, the distribution of business is to change as a result of decisions on the part of the defendant, then only those cases where the defendant is actually given a choice of venue for his trial are relevant: defendants who have no say in the matter cannot effect any changes—in such cases the change must come from the prosecution or the judiciary. The main focus of attention must therefore be upon those defendants who reported having been given an option of venue for their trial and their reasons for making a particular choice, although those who chose summary trial at a magistrates' court, but were sent to the Crown Court for sentence, are not, of course, adding to the volume of Crown Court business by their own actions.

3.1 The plea

The most outstanding feature of the three groups who chose the venue for their trial themselves, is the difference in the distribution of guilty pleas and not guilty pleas. It will be seen later that the reasons defendants gave for making a particular choice of venue for their trial reflect and support the plea they entered.

Table 5 *Distribution of guilty and not guilty pleas among the three groups of defendants who chose the venue for their trial*

	Venue for trial chosen by defendant			
	Crown Court		Magistrates' court	
	Disposal at			
	Crown Court		Magistrates' court	Crown Court
Plea	Actual plea	Original intention	Actual plea	Actual plea
	%	%	%	%
Not guilty to all charges	69	85	6	—
Guilty to all charges	22	6	88	95
Mixed plea	9	9	6	5
All defendants who chose the venue for their trial: base	166 = 100%	166 = 100%	203 = 100%	43 = 100%

Table 5 shows the venue for trial that was chosen by the defendant, and the plea entered against the charges. For defendants who chose to go to the Crown Court for trial the plea that they originally intended to make at the time they made their venue decision is also shown. Information about the plea originally intended was obtained because it was thought there might be some defendants whose original intention was to plead not guilty at the Crown Court, but who for various reasons eventually pleaded guilty. It was hoped that in this way it would be possible to explain the somewhat anomalous presence of any 'guilty-plea' defendants at the Crown Court.

Of the 166 defendants who chose trial on indictment at the Crown Court, 69 per cent reported pleading not guilty to all the charges against them, while of the 203 defendants who had chosen to have their cases heard by magistrates and whose cases were finally disposed of by the magistrates' court, only 6 per cent had pleaded not guilty to all charges. None of the 43 defendants who had elected summary trial at a magistrates' court but who were sent to the Crown Court for sentence contested all the charges against them.

Of the 36 defendants who chose trial on indictment at the Crown Court and who pleaded guilty to all the charges when they appeared at the Crown Court, 26 had decided to plead guilty only after they had made their venue decision. This means that of the 166 defendants who chose to go before a judge and jury at the Crown Court 85 per cent made their decision with the intention of pleading not guilty.

3.2 Reasons for choosing trial on indictment at the Crown Court or summary trial at a magistrates' court

Having noted the marked difference in the distribution of guilty and not guilty pleas at the two levels of court we find when we look at the reasons defendants gave for

Table 6 *Reasons for choosing trial on indictment at the Crown Court given by defendants who, at the time they made their venue decision, intended pleading not guilty to all the charges against them, and by defendants who intended pleading guilty to some or all of the charges against them[1]*

Reasons for choosing trial on indictment at the Crown Court	Intended plea		All defendants choosing Crown Court trial
	Not guilty to all charges	Guilty to some or all charges	
	%	%	%
The case is gone into more thoroughly: a better hearing	55	64	57
There is a jury to listen to the case	49	32[2]	46
On solicitor's advice	40	36	40
Magistrates' court is a 'police court': biased	36	28	35
Better chance of being acquitted	33	12	30
Judges are better qualified (than magistrates) to hear a case	17	36	20
To take advantage of the delay in coming to court	12	16	13
Better chance of a light sentence	9	8	8
Can be represented in court	9	4	8
On police advice	2	—	2
To find out the case for the prosecution	—	8	1
Other answers	10	4	9
All defendants choosing Crown Court trial: base	141 = 100%	25 = 100%	166 = 100%

[1] The plea that defendants originally intended entering against charges at the time they made their venue decision has been used in this table. This is felt to be more relevant to the reasons defendants gave for making a particular choice of venue than the actual, and sometimes different, plea that was entered when the defendant subsequently appeared in court.
[2] Only one defendant gave this as a reason for choosing trial on indictment and always intended pleading guilty to the charges against him.

Table 7 *Reasons for electing summary trial at a magistrates' court given by defendants whose cases were tried and disposed of by magistrates according to the plea entered against the charges, and for all defendants whose cases were tried at the magistrates' court but who were committed by the magistrates to the Crown Court for sentence*

Reasons for electing summary trial at a magistrates' court	At magistrates' court for			
	Trial and disposal			Trial only
	Pleaded			
	Guilty to all charges	Not guilty to some/all charges	All defendants	All defendants
	%	%	%	%
Get the case to court quickly	41	29	40	53
Better chance of a light sentence	29	28	30	49
Get the trial over quickly	17	8	16	9
Not important/serious enough for Crown Court	15	17	14	14
Cheap: including 'don't have to employ a solicitor'	10	13	10	2
On police advice	10	—	9	7
'Get it over'—not explained	9	4	9	7
To avoid being remanded	6	8	6	16
On solicitor's advice	6	25	8	5
Did not want a jury	4	21	6	2
Save taxpayers' money	4	4	4	5
Avoid publicity	4	4	4	—
Case is gone into more thoroughly: fairer	2	—	2	7
Less formidable/less fuss	3	4	3	—
Better chance of being acquitted	1	8	1	—
On someone else's advice	2	—	2	2
Other answers	4	8	5	7
All defendants electing trial at a magistrates' court: base	179 = 100%	24 = 100%	203 = 100%	43 = 100%

choosing a particular venue for their trial, that not only do the reasons reflect and support the plea, but they also show that those defendants who went to the Crown Court for trial had a very different type of concern about their trial, compared with those who had chosen summary trial at a magistrates' court.

It has been mentioned previously that the tight timetable for this survey imposed certain restrictions on what could be done, including the size of samples that could be approached for interview. This in turn has limited the number of factors providing groups of sufficient size for analysis. For example, we acknowledge that a defendant's attitude to his trial and the reasons he gives in retrospect for having made a particular choice of venue are likely to be influenced not only by the plea he made in answer to the charges, but also by the outcome of his case; this is especially likely in cases where a defendant pleads not guilty. However only 22 defendants chose to be tried by magistrates and pleaded not guilty to some or all of the charges against them, and to further sub-divide this group into those acquitted and those convicted would provide groups with too few defendants to make meaningful comparisons with the comparable groups at the Crown Court. It has therefore been necessary to use either plea *or* verdict as a variable for analysis, whichever is most appropriate, and not a combined plea-verdict factor. However, it should be noted that defendants who chose summary trial at a magistrates' court but were then committed to the Crown Court for sentence, are by definition a group in which all 43 defendants were convicted.[1]

[1] Tables C2 and C3, p 76, show the proportions of defendants in each of the three groups who chose the venue for their trial who were convicted of some or all of the charges against them.

Tables 6 and 7 show the reasons given for choosing trial at the Crown Court by those defendants whose cases were tried and disposed of at the Crown Court and the reasons for electing summary trial at a magistrates' court given by those defendants whose cases were disposed of by the magistrates, and by those defendants who were committed from the magistrates' court to the Crown Court for sentence only.

3.2.1 *Reasons for choosing trial on indictment at the Crown Court*

Table 6 shows that for all 166 defendants who chose to go to the Crown Court for trial the main reasons for doing so were in order to have a more thorough hearing of the case, reported by 57 per cent of defendants, and to have a jury listen to the case and decide upon a verdict rather than have the decision rest with one or more magistrates, reported by 46 per cent of defendants. Both these reasons are obviously linked to the concern of these defendants to have the best chance of acquittal, and further analysis (table 6) showed that, as would be expected, defendants who intended pleading not guilty to all the charges against them were more likely than defendants who intended pleading guilty to at least one of the charges against them, to have chosen trial at the Crown Court because they believed they would stand a better chance of acquittal.

Of the 166 defendants who chose Crown Court trial 40 per cent reported making such a choice because they were advised to do so by a solicitor. The reasons the solicitors gave in support of their advice were not recorded at this question, and are not included in this table but are discussed separately in the following chapter.

Included in the category of other answers—9 per cent of all defendants choosing Crown Court trial—are three defendants who went to the Crown Court because they thought it would be easier to get bail; they felt that pleading guilty at a magistrates' court would lead automatically to a remand in custody. Going to the Crown Court for the experience, and as a deliberate attempt to waste the time and money of the police, were reasons given by only two defendants. One defendant wanted the anonymity of trial at the Crown Court, rather than going before magistrates who were familiar both with him and his family, and only one defendant chose to go to the Crown Court because he was sure he would be sent up for sentence anyway. Three defendants, all of whom intended pleading not guilty to all the charges against them, chose trial on indictment at the Crown Court because it had been recommended to them by someone other than the police or their solicitor.[1]

Of the 141 defendants who when they made their choice of venue, intended pleading not guilty to all the charges against them, 12 per cent (17 defendants) wanted to take advantage of the probable delay in their case getting to court. Nine reported that they wanted the delay in order to have time to prepare their case, and the remaining eight defendants in the group said they had wanted the delay for other reasons. All those defendants who chose Crown Court trial with the intention of pleading guilty to at least some of the charges against them, and who gave as reason in support of their choice the advantages of the probable delay in their case getting to court, wanted time for reasons other than to prepare their defence. These other reasons for wanting a delay included having time to stay with a pregnant wife, having time to look after a dying father, and having time to continue running a business. Two defendants were subject to suspended sentences, and were under the impression that if the period of suspension had elapsed by the time they got to court for trial, the suspended sentence could not be brought into force. One defendant explained his reasons for choosing Crown Court trial at length: he told the interviewer that defendants who, like himself, are sure they will be convicted and be given a prison sentence sometimes deliberately delay their trial in the hope that when the judge sees how long they have been waiting on remand, he will be more lenient and inclined to pass a lighter sentence.

Time on remand counts towards the eventual sentence, and is apparently regarded as an easy option compared with time served after conviction. The technique adopted to ensure maximum delay is as follows: assure counsel that a plea of guilty is going to be made, then on appearing at court plead not guilty. Counsel, having no case prepared, then withdraws, and the case is adjourned to a later date. This 'technique' had been learned during previous imprisonment, and the interviewer was assured that fellow

---

[1] For a further discussion of the advice given to defendants regarding the venue for trial see chapter 4.

prisoners had done and would continue to do likewise. However the reasons that the majority of defendants in the group gave for choosing trial at the Crown Court seem to be reasonable and consistent with the plea they entered: very few would seem to have had such ulterior motives.

3.2.2 *Reasons for electing summary trial at a magistrates' court*

From table 7 it is apparent that the two groups of defendants who chose to go to a magistrates' court for their trial were concerned with rather different aspects of their case compared with those who had chosen trial on indictment at the Crown Court.

This is not so surprising when it is remembered that the majority of defendants who chose to be tried by magistrates pleaded guilty, while the majority of defendants who chose to go to the Crown Court for trial did so at least with the intention of pleading not guilty. Defendants who elected summary trial at a magistrates' court did so, firstly because they wanted to be dealt with as soon as possible, and secondly, possibly acknowledging their guilt, because they wanted the lightest possible sentence.

Of the 203 defendants who elected trial at a magistrates' court and whose cases were finally disposed of by the magistrates, 40 per cent wanted to be dealt with summarily at a magistrates' court because they were anxious to get their case to court quickly, and 30 per cent of this group of defendants thought they had the better chance of light sentence at a magistrates' court.

The pattern is similar for those 43 defendants who after choosing trial at a magistrates' court were committed to the Crown Court for sentence: 53 per cent chose summary trial at a magistrates' court because they wanted to get their case to court quickly, and 49 per cent elected trial at a magistrates' court for the improved chances of a light sentence.[1]

Only one defendant in each of these two groups who chose to go to a magistrates' court for trial thought the Crown Court was a 'police court', in that the evidence offered by the police would be believed in preference to the evidence put forward by a defendant, and this reason is included in the category of 'other answers'. However the majority of reasons in this category concern defendants who felt there was no point in doing anything else as they were pleading guilty. One defendant, whose case was tried and disposed of by magistrates, said that he would have preferred Crown Court trial as he thought he would have been given a lighter sentence. However he had elected summary trial at a magistrates' court because he thought that had he chosen to go to the Crown Court his eight co-defendants would have been sent up with him, and they, in his opinion, would have been convicted and would have received custodial sentences.

It can be seen from table 7 that there are significant differences in the frequency with which certain reasons were reported by defendants who pleaded guilty to all charges and by defendants who pleaded not guilty to some or all of the charges against them.

Defendants who contested any of the charges against them were more likely to have chosen trial at a magistrates' court on the advice of a solicitor[2], and also because they had not wanted to appear before a jury. The reasons given for not wanting to appear before a jury were varied, and, as is evident from the fact that this reason was also mentioned by some defendants who pleaded guilty to all charges, were sometimes based on a misunderstanding of court procedure. The explanations included not liking a jury 'knowing my affairs', and conversely, a jury 'not knowing enough about me, my home background, and what made me do it'. Some defendants said they would be frightened by having to appear before a jury, and some thought the jury would be prejudiced against them. Also mentioned as a reason for avoiding a jury was having to pay the expenses of the jurors, whatever the outcome.

---

[1] In table 7 we have shown as three separate categories those defendants who wanted to 'get the case to court quickly', those who wanted to 'get the trial over quickly' and those who simply said that they wanted 'to get it over with'. If these three categories are combined we find that 57 per cent of the 203 defendants whose cases were disposed of at magistrates' courts, and 65 per cent of 43 defendants who were tried by magistrates, but where committed to the Crown Court for sentence, were concerned that there should be no delay at any stage of their trial.
[2] For a further discussion of the advice given to defendants regarding the venue for trial see chapter 4.

3.2.3 A comparison of the reasons given by defendants for choosing either Crown Court trial, or trial at a magistrates' court

For all three groups who chose the venue for their own trial the analysis has shown that the main reasons given by defendants to support the choice they made are associated with the plea that was entered by the majority of defendants in the group.

The main reasons for going to the Crown Court, where 85 per cent of defendants originally intended pleading not guilty to all charges, relate to what was seen as the improved chance of acquittal, while at magistrates' courts, where less than 10 per cent of either group actually pleaded not guilty to all charges, the main reasons relate to having the case finished in the shortest time with the minimum penalty and expense.

Table 7 shows that very few defendants chose to be tried at a magistrates' court because they believed they would have an improved chance of acquittal, and this reflects the small number of defendants who were prepared to bring a contested case before magistrates. One indication of why this might have been is shown in table 6 by the considerable proportion of defendants who gave as a reason for choosing trial at the Crown Court, their desire to avoid the magistrates' courts which they felt to be 'police courts'—there was thought to be a bias by the magistrates towards the evidence given by the police in preference to that put forward by the accused or his defending counsel; of the 166 defendants who chose to go to the Crown Court 35 per cent gave this as at least one of their reasons.

It is apparent from tables 6 and 7 that the same reasons were sometimes mentioned both by the group of defendants who chose trial at the Crown Court, and by those who chose trial at a magistrates' court. 'Having a more thorough hearing' was the most frequently mentioned reason for choosing trial at the Crown Court, but was one of the most infrequent reasons given for electing to stay for trial at a magistrates' court, and it could therefore be assumed to have been of relatively minor importance to those who chose to have their cases heard by magistrates. The 'better chance of a light sentence' was the second most frequently mentioned reason for electing trial at a magistrates' court, but was only mentioned infrequently by those who chose to be tried at the Crown Court, and hence appears to have been a minor consideration to this group of defendants. However it should be remembered that while the most favourable outcome for defendants who plead guilty is a light sentence, the most favourable outcome for defendants who plead not guilty is an acquittal. The differences in priority attached to having the best chance of a light sentence between those who chose to be tried by magistrates and those who chose to be tried before Crown Court judges are therefore strongly associated with the differences in the proportions of defendants pleading guilty at these two levels of court.

The relationship between plea and venue is illustrated further by analysis which shows that of the 179 defendants who chose to be tried at a magistrates' court, who pleaded guilty to all the charges against them and whose cases were finally disposed of at the magistrates' court, 50 per cent said they would have made a different choice and chosen to go to a Crown Court for trial had they been contesting any of the charges.

A similar proportion of those who were committed to the Crown Court for sentence, after choosing to be tried by magistrates, would also have chosen Crown Court trial had they been pleading not guilty.

Table 5 shows that there were 13 defendants who contested all the charges against them and who nevertheless elected summary trial at a magistrates' court, and that 10 defendants chose Crown Court trial with the intention of pleading guilty to all charges. The following section considers the reasons why these few defendants made a venue decision contrary to what would be expected on the basis of their plea.

3.2.4 Defendants who chose trial at the Crown Court and intended pleading guilty to all charges: 10 defendants

It would appear from their answers that eight of these 10 defendants had been prepared to go to the Crown Court with a plea of guilty because they believed that for various reasons judgement would be fairer at the higher court.

Six of the 10 chose Crown Court trial because they said they had more confidence in a professionally qualified judge than in a magistrate. Comments included, 'a judge is more experienced and will take an interest in your case and listen to the circumstances', 'a judge is trained and won't be against me because of my appearance—a magistrate is unpaid and untrained'.

One defendant wanted to avoid a particular magistrate who he believed always sent people to prison, so he thought by going to the Crown Court he would get a lighter sentence. He was fined £100.

Two defendants followed their solicitor's advice: one reported being told that he would be sent to the Crown Court for sentence anyway, and the other reported that he had been told he would get a lighter sentence from the Crown Court judge.

The remaining defendant presented a rather confused argument: he thought that pleading guilty at a magistrates' court would lead to a remand in custody, but at the Crown Court he would be released on bail pending trial. He added that as he was subject to a suspended sentence, he would 'have to go' to the Crown Court for sentence, even if he chose a magistrates' court for trial.

3.2.5 *Defendants who chose trial at a magistrates' court and pleaded not guilty to all charges: 13 defendants*

It is rather difficult to account for the presence of some of this group of defendants at magistrates' courts, as the reasons they gave to support their venue decision do not generally explain why their priorities were so different from those of other defendants who were contesting the charges against them, and who chose trial on indictment at the Crown Court.

Four of these 13 defendants wanted their cases dealt with quickly, but for only two can we find possible explanations as to why this aspect took on such importance: one was an unmarried mother who had a child to look after and could not afford to be away from her job—she needed the money to be able to keep her child, the other defendant had a very pregnant wife whom he did not want to leave alone while he was at court. Three defendants thought their offences were too trivial to take before a judge and jury—two were very minor cases of shoplifting by elderly people, and the third was a charge of assault occasioning actual bodily harm. Four defendants thought that at the magistrates' court they stood the better chance of acquittal, or, if they were convicted, of a lighter sentence. One defendant, a young Indian boy, did not know anything about the different court systems, so could not really make a choice, but he did say that the police had advised him to plead guilty 'to get it over with'. He contested the charges and was acquitted.

3.3 Reasons for choosing a particular venue for trial given by defendants who had previous convictions recorded against them, and by those who reported having no previous convictions

The previous section discussed the reasons defendants gave for choosing a particular venue for their trial and the relationship between both the choice and the reasons given and the plea that was entered in answer to the charges. The following section considers whether defendants who had a previous criminal record, and had therefore probably experienced at least one type of court, chose a particular venue for their trial for reasons different from those defendants who had no previous convictions recorded against them.[1]

Table 8 shows the proportions of defendants in each of the three groups who chose the venue for their trial, who reported having previous convictions recorded against them.

Among the group who chose to appear at a magistrates' court but who were committed to the Crown Court for sentence, all but one defendant reported having previous convictions recorded against them. This group is therefore excluded from the following discussion, since it would not be meaningful to consider their reasons for choosing summary trial at a magistrates' court on the basis of previous record. However, such a

---

[1] It should be noted that some 'previous offenders' may never have appeared at a court before as a defendant, since for some minor offences, especially traffic violations, it is possible to be convicted without ever making an appearance at court. Similarly, if a defendant reported having no previous convictions it may not always have meant that this was his first appearance at court, he may have been previously charged with offences but found not guilty and discharged. However, the previous experience that defendants had of the two levels of court, both as defendants and in other capacities, is discussed later, see chapter 5.

Table 8 *Proportions of defendants who chose the venue for their trial with previous convictions (numbers and percentages)*

Previous criminal record	Venue for trial chosen by defendant					
	Crown Court		Magistrates' court			
	Disposal at					
	Crown Court		Magistrates' court		Crown Court	
	Nos	%	Nos	%	Nos	%
No previous convictions	37	22	77	38	1	2
Previous convictions	129	78	126	62	42	98
All defendants who chose the venue for their trial: base	166	100	203	100	43	100

high proportion of previous offenders among this group is not unexpected, since committal for sentence usually requires a defendant to have a record.

3.3.1 *Those who chose trial on indictment at the Crown Court*

Table 9 shows the reasons for choosing trial on indictment at the Crown Court, given by defendants who had previous convictions recorded against them, and by those who reported having no previous record.

The table shows that 'previous offenders' were in fact more likely than defendants who reported having no previous convictions to mention certain reasons for having chosen to go for trial at the Crown Court, and that these particular reasons seem to relate to a previous experience at a magistrates' court. For example, 'previous offenders' were more likely to have chosen to go for Crown Court trial because their case would be dealt with more thoroughly, and because the magistrates' court is thought to be biased.

Table 9 *Reasons for choosing trial on indictment at the Crown Court given by those defendants who had no previous criminal record and by those who had previous convictions*

| Reasons for choosing trial on indictment at the Crown Court | No previous convictions | Previous convictions | All choosing Crown Court trial |
	%	%	%
The case is gone into more thoroughly: a better hearing	32	64	57
There is a jury to listen to the case	38	49	46
On solicitor's advice	68	32	40
Magistrates' court is a 'police court': biased	16	40	35
Better chance of being acquitted	30	30	30
Judges are better qualified (than magistrates) to hear a case	11	22	20
To take advantage of the delay in coming to court	5	15	13
Better chance of a light sentence	3	10	8
Can be represented in court	3	10	8
On police advice	3	2	2
To find out the case for the prosecution	—	2	1
Other answers	3	11	9
All defendants choosing trial at the Crown Court: base	37 = 100%	129 = 100%	166 = 100%

'Previous offenders' were also more likely than defendants with no previous record to want to go to the Crown Court in order to take advantage of the probable delay in their case getting to court.[1]

Defendants who had no previous convictions, however, appeared to take more note of the advice of a solicitor. This was the reason mentioned most frequently by this sub-group, and was given by a significantly greater proportion of defendants with no previous convictions, than by 'previous offenders'. Further analysis showed that of defendants who had previous convictions recorded against them, those who had also served a custodial sentence were even less likely than those who had no experience of a custodial sentence, to mention 'solicitor's advice' as a reason for choosing Crown Court trial: of the 69 defendants who had previously served a custodial sentence, only 19 per cent reported that the advice of a solicitor had been one reason why they had chosen Crown Court trial, whereas of the 60 defendants who, although they had previous convictions had not served a custodial sentence, 47 per cent reported the same reason for choosing Crown Court trial.

It was thought originally that these differences might be accounted for by differences in the frequency with which these three sub-groups consulted a solicitor for advice concerning the venue for their trial. The table below shows that in fact the only significant difference was between those defendants who had no previous convictions, and those who had served a custodial sentence: defendants with no previous convictions were more likely to have consulted a solicitor concerning the venue for their trial. It could therefore be concluded that the differences in the frequency with which 'solicitor's advice' was mentioned as a reason for choosing Crown Court trial by these three sub-groups of defendants is only partially explained by differences in the frequency with which solicitors were consulted for advice concerning the venue option, and it might be that the more experience a defendant has of the legal/penal system the less weight is he likely to attach to the advice of his solicitor; he knows the arguments for and against making a particular choice of venue from his own previous experience.

3.3.2 *Those who elected summary trial at a magistrates' court, and whose cases were finally disposed of by the magistrates*

Table 11 shows that as with those defendants who chose Crown Court trial, there were considerable differences in the frequency with which certain reasons for choosing summary trial at a magistrates' court were mentioned by defendants, dependent upon whether or not they had previous convictions recorded against them.

Table 10 *Proportions of defendants with previous convictions who discussed the venue for their trial with a solicitor and who chose to go for trial at the Crown Court*

	Defendant had					
	No previous convictions		Previous convictions			
			with a custodial sentence		with no custodial sentence	
	Nos	%	Nos	%	Nos	%
Defendant discussed venue with a solicitor	31	88	50	72	50	83
All defendants who chose Crown Court trial: base[2]	34	100	69	100	60	100

[1] Of the 19 defendants who had previous convictions and wanted to take advantage of the delay in their case coming to court, eight wanted the delay in order to have time to prepare their case, and 11 wanted the delay for other reasons. Of the two defendants with no previous convictions who wanted a delay, one wanted time to prepare his case and the other wanted the delay for other reasons. These 'other reasons' have been discussed previously, see 3.2.1.

[2] Excludes those not answering.

Table 11 *Reasons for choosing trial at a magistrates' court given by those defendants who had previous convictions and by those who had no previous criminal record—those whose cases were tried and disposed of by magistrates*

Reasons for choosing summary trial at a magistrates' court	No previous convictions	Previous convictions	All choosing trial at a magistrates' court
	%	%	%
Get the case to court quickly	35	42	40
Better chance of a light sentence	13	41	30
Get the trial over quickly	19	14	16
Not important/serious enough for Crown Court	23	9	14
Cheap: including 'don't have to employ a solicitor'	8	12	10
On police advice	14	6	9
'Get it over'—not explained	14	6	9
To avoid being remanded	1	9	6
On solicitor's advice	5	10	8
Did not want a jury	5	7	6
Save taxpayer's money	4	4	4
Avoid publicity	9	1	4
Case is gone into more thoroughly: fairer	—	3	2
Less formidable/less fuss	6	1	3
Better chance of being acquitted	—	2	1
On someone else's advice	3	2	2
Other answers	8	2	5
All defendants electing trial at a magistrates' court: base	78 = 100%	125 = 100%	203 = 100%

Not surprisingly, defendants who had been previously convicted of some offence were more concerned with the outcome of their case: this group, compared with those who had no previous convictions, mentioned significantly more often that they had chosen to be tried by magistrates because they thought they had the better chance of a light sentence at the lower court. Further analysis showed that of all defendants who had previous convictions, among those who had previously served a custodial sentence the better chance of a light sentence was mentioned more often than by defendants who although they had a record had never served a custodial sentence: of the 43 defendants who had served custodial sentences 53 per cent had chosen summary trial at a magistrates' court for the improved chances of a light sentence, while of the 82 defendants who had previous convictions but had never served a sentence only 34 per cent mentioned this same reason.

The analysis also showed that defendants who had previous convictions irrespective of whether they had ever served a custodial sentence were more likely than defendants with no record to mention that they had chosen to be tried by magistrates in order to avoid being remanded. However, defendants who had no previous convictions were more likely to have chosen trial at a magistrates' court because they did not regard their case as sufficiently serious to merit going to the Crown Court.

On this evidence it seems that among defendants who chose summary trial at a magistrates' court, those who had previous convictions were, not unreasonably, more concerned with the outcome of their trial—getting a light sentence, and in some cases avoiding what would have been a return to custody, while defendants with no previous record showed some concern with the wider issues of their case.

If the right-hand column of table 7 is compared with table 11, it is clear that the distribution of reasons given by defendants who were subsequently sent to the Crown Court for sentence resembles quite closely that for defendants whose cases were tried and disposed of at the magistrates' court and who had previous convictions recorded against them. This is as would be expected since all defendants who were sent up for sentence by magistrates to the Crown Court, with the exception of one, reported that they had been previously convicted of some criminal offence.

3.4 Second thoughts on the venue decision

At the end of the interview defendants were asked whether, if they could go back and choose again, they would make the same or a different venue decision.
At various stages during the interview, as more was learnt about the circumstances of a defendant's offence and his trial, defendants had been asked whether, if particular circumstances had been different, their venue decision would have remained the same. In the following section these particular aspects of the trial and their possible effects on the venue decision are considered, together with an examination of what might have been the effects of those changed decisions on the distribution of these cases between the two levels of court.

It has already been noted that about one-half of both groups of defendants who had chosen summary trial at a magistrates' court and had pleaded guilty to all charges against them, would have preferred Crown Court trial had they been contesting any or all of the charges. It was also found that of the 26 defendants who had chosen Crown Court trial with the intention of pleading not guilty but had eventually pleaded guilty at the higher court only nine said they would have preferred to have been tried at a magistrates' court had they known that eventually they would plead guilty at the Crown Court.

Analysis showed that of the 166 defendants who chose to go for trial at the Crown Court 20 per cent said that at the time they had made their venue decision, if they had known how long they were going to have to wait before their case came up they would have preferred to have been tried before a magistrates' court.

Table 12 shows how long these defendants estimated that they would have to wait before their case came up at the Crown Court.

Table 12 *Waiting period for case to come up at the Crown Court estimated by those defendants who chose to go for trial at the Crown Court*

Estimated waiting period	%
Up to 1 month	12
1 month to less than 2 months	14
2 months to less than 4 months	25
4 months to less than 6 months	14
6 months or longer	35
All defendants choosing trial at the Crown Court: base[1]	156 = 100%

It is interesting to note that over one-third of this group of defendants anticipated a wait of six months or longer. Defendants who pleaded guilty to some or all of the charges against them were no more likely than defendants who pleaded not guilty to the charges to want summary trial at a magistrates' court because of the anticipated delay, or to estimate that they would have a shorter waiting period before their case came up.

Although it is not possible to show the accuracy of defendants' estimates, table C8, Appendix C, shows that by 20 weeks after committal to the Crown Court over one-half of the 'guilty-plea' cases had been disposed of, whereas it took just over 28 weeks to dispose of half the contested cases.[2] Analysis also showed that defendants who said they would have chosen summary trial had they known how long they would have to wait before their case came up, in the event did not wait significantly longer between

---

[1] Excludes those not answering.
[2] Tables C8, C9 and C10, pp 78 and 79, show for each of the three groups of defendants who chose the venue for their trial, how long they had to wait for their cases to be disposed of by the courts.

the committal of their case and its disposal than defendants who would still opt for Crown Court trial. It could be concluded therefore that for some defendants even a comparatively short period between committal and disposal was regarded as too long a wait, while for others the protracted period was not seen as sufficient inconvenience to merit wanting a different venue for trial.

Of the 166 defendants who chose Crown Court trial 35 per cent said that had they known or thought that they were going to be remanded in custody waiting for their case to come up they would have preferred to have had their case heard at a magistrates' court; 17 per cent of this group of 166 defendants had in fact been remanded in custody awaiting trail.

Although the analyses of answers to these questions suggest that a possible way of attempting to reduce the volume of business at Crown Courts might be to inform defendants of the delays they could expect or the likelihood of a custodial remand if they choose to go for trial at the Crown Court, before they made their venue decision, it should be remembered that the evidence from this study shows that defendants are choosing Crown Court trial because they believe they will get a fairer and more thorough hearing at the higher court and because they believe that in that way they will have the best chance of acquittal—given that they contest the charges against them. To attract defendants to summary trial at a magistrates' court it would seem therefore that such courts must be seen to provide the fair trial and thorough hearing that is at present associated with Crown Courts, and defendants should not be expected to sacrifice what they see as the best chance of a fair trial for a quick appearance at court.

Not surprisingly however, one great attraction to magistrates' courts would be the presence of a jury. Defendants who chose Crown Court trial were asked whether they would have elected summary trial if there had been a jury to listen to their case at the lower court. Under these conditions 71 per cent of the 166 defendants who chose Crown Court trial said that they would have opted to go to a magistrates' court instead. Those who chose summary trial at a magistrates' court were asked the corresponding question: if they could have been tried at the Crown Court *without* there being a jury would they have wanted to have their case heard there? Remembering that for the majority of defendants such a situation would have been possible had they continued to plead guilty, 12 per cent of the 203 defendants whose cases were tried and disposed of by magistrates, and 21 per cent of the 43 defendants who had subsequently been sentenced by Crown Court judges would have made a different venue decision and chosen Crown Court trial.[1]

At the end of the interview, when defendants had possibly become more aware of the differences between the courts, and had been thinking about the choice they had made and its results they were asked whether, if they could go back and choose again, they would make the same choice or whether they would make a different venue decision. Table 13 shows an analysis of answers to this question.

There was a considerable affirmation of faith in the Crown Court to deal fairly and justly with offenders; 85 per cent of those who chose to go to the Crown Court said they would make the same choice again. Moreover, only 10 per cent of those who had pleaded not guilty to all the charges against them would now choose summary trial at a magistrates' court. Of the 10 defendants who chose Crown Court trial with the intention of pleading guilty to all the charges against them, nine confirmed that they would still make the same choice of venue for their trial; only one defendant from this group now wished he had been dealt with at a magistrates' court.[2] The two principal reasons for now wanting summary trial at a magistrates' court were to avoid delay at any stage of the hearing, 74 per cent of defendants gave this reason, and the hope of getting a lighter sentence, 57 per cent of defendants mentioned this reason. It is interesting to note that eight of the 23 defendants who now wanted summary trial at a magistrates' court said that this was because they did not want to appear before a jury.

Although the proportion of defendants who had chosen trial at the Crown Court and now wished they had opted for summary trial at a magistrates' court is small and

---

[1] For a discussion of the possible effects of improved knowledge of the two court systems by defendants on the distribution of cases between the two courts, see chapter 6, p 37.
[2] See table C4, p 77.

Table 13 *Now that the case is over, if defendants could choose again, what choice of venue for their trial would they make?*

Venue for trial that defendant would choose now that the case is over	Venue for trial chosen by defendant					
	Crown Court		Magistrates' court			
	Disposal at					
	Crown Court		Magistrates' court		Crown Court	
	Nos	%	Nos	%	Nos	%
Crown Court	137	85	29	14	21	49
Magistrates' court	23	14	168	83	21	49
Would not matter/not bothered	2	1	6	3	1	2
All defendants who chose the venue for their trial: base[1]	162	100	203	100	43	100

would on its own have made little difference to the total amount of business in the Crown Court, the dissatisfaction with trial at a magistrates' court and the readiness of this group to go to the Crown Court must also be studied. There does not appear to be a large volume of dissatisfaction; only 14 per cent of the 203 defendants who chose summary trial and whose cases were disposed of by magistrates, now wished that they had chosen trial at the Crown Court, and only one of these was from the group of 13 defendants who had contested all the charges against them at the lower court.

It is particularly interesting to find that 12 defendants who chose trial at a magistrates' court now wanted to go for trial at the Crown Court because they believed there was a better chance of a light sentence at the higher court. Thirteen defendants thought they would have a more thorough hearing at the Crown Court, and six defendants particularly wanted a jury—this would not of course have been possible unless they had changed their plea to one of not guilty.

The greatest volume of dissatisfaction was amongst those who having chosen summary trial at a magistrates' court had then been sent up to the Crown Court for sentence: about one-half of this group of defendants would now choose Crown Court trial; the principal reason was to get a more thorough hearing, but several defendants wanted Crown Court trial because they could be represented in court.

If the two main groups of defendants whose cases were heard and disposed of at the venue of their choice and who would now make a different decision regarding the venue for their trial are considered, then, on the basis of the sample numbers involved it would appear at first sight that the business of the Crown Court would be only marginally increased, had it been possible for defendants to have acted on their second thoughts. However, it should be remembered that differential sampling fractions were applied when selecting defendants from the two levels of court. Defendants whose cases were tried and disposed of at magistrates' courts were selected over a three day period from a random selection of half the magistrates' courts in the Greater London area, while defendants appearing for trial at Crown Court centres were selected over a 10 day period from all the Crown Court centres in the same area dealing with criminal business. It can therefore be estimated that a factor of x7 should be applied to the sample of defendants whose cases were tried and disposed of at magistrates' courts if the sample of this business is to correspond to that of a sample of business from the Crown Court. Applying this factor of x7 to those defendants whose cases were tried and disposed of by magistrates and who now wished they had chosen to go for trial at the Crown Court, and considering these 'second thoughts' as in fact operational, it can be seen that, on balance, the Crown Court would then have had a marked increase in the volume of business. Although such a situation is hypothetical, it does

[1] Excludes those not answering.

perhaps indicate the possible venue decisions that might be made by these particular defendants were they to be brought to court on some future occasion, and it illustrates the implications for the case-loads of the two levels of court. Bearing in mind that the probability of appearing at court is much greater for those who have made previous appearances than for those never previously charged, then this trend gives cause for continuing concern.

4   Advice to the defendant

In discussing the reasons defendants gave for choosing a particular venue for their trial it was apparent that for some defendants the decision was, at least in part, the result of advice they had been given. The principal sources of this advice were solicitors and the police, and the following chapter discusses the role of these two groups, the advice they gave and the extent to which it was acted upon in relation to the defendant's venue decision.

4.1 The role of solicitors

Table 6 showed that of the 166 defendants who chose to go to the Crown Court for their trial 40 per cent spontaneously mentioned that the advice they had been given by a solicitor had been one reason why they had made that particular choice. Because of the form this question took this was likely to be an underestimate of the total number of defendants who had approached a solicitor for advice concerning their case. When asked the specific question, a much higher proportion of defendants said that they had in fact spoken to a solicitor about where their case should be heard.

Table 14 shows the numbers of defendants in each of the three groups who chose the venue for their trial, after discussing it with a solicitor.

Table 14 *Proportions of defendants in each of the three groups who chose the venue for their trial after discussing it with a solicitor (numbers and percentages)*

	Venue for trial chosen by defendant					
	Crown Court		Magistrates' court			
	Disposal at					
	Crown Court		Magistrates' court		Crown Court	
	Nos	%	Nos	%	Nos	%
Defendant talked to a solicitor about the venue for trial	130	78	34	17	8	19
All defendants who chose the venue for their trial: base	166	100	203	100	43	100

It can be seen from these tables that defendants who chose Crown Court trial were far more likely to have talked to a solicitor about where their case should be heard than either of the two groups who elected summary trial at a magistrates' court. But for all three groups who discussed the venue with a solicitor the majority made a choice which was in agreement with the advice of their solicitor.

Of the 166 defendants who chose to go to the Crown Court for trial, 78 per cent had discussed where they should have their case heard with a solicitor, and of these 130, 85 per cent were advised by their solicitor to ask for trial at the Crown Court, 2 per cent were advised to opt for summary trial at a magistrates' court, and the remaining 13 per cent were not given any specific recommendation, but were told about the differences between the two levels of court.

Table 15 *Proportions of defendants who followed the advice they had been given by their solicitor when they chose the venue for their trial (numbers and percentages)*

Venue recommended by solicitor	Venue for trial chosen by defendant				
	Crown Court		Magistrates' court		
	Disposal at				
	Crown Court		Magistrates' court		Crown Court
	Nos	%	Nos	%	Nos only
Crown Court	110	85	4	12	(1)
Magistrates' court	3	2	23	68	(6)
No particular venue recommended	17	13	7	20	(1)
All discussing venue with solicitor and choosing venue for their trial: base	130	100	34	100	(8)

( ) Denotes number not percentage.

Of the 110 defendants who were advised by their solicitor to go to the Crown Court for trial, 15 per cent were not given any reasons or explanation to support the advice, and two of the three defendants advised to stay for trial at a magistrates' court said that the solicitor had failed to explain why he thought this was the best course of action.

Of the 203 defendants who chose trial at a magistrates' court and whose cases were tried and disposed of by the magistrates, only 17 per cent discussed with a solicitor where their case should be heard. Of these 34, 68 per cent were advised to stay and be tried by magistrates, and 12 per cent to opt to go for trial at a higher court before a judge and jury. A venue for trial was not recommended by the solicitor to the remaining defendants: an explanation of the differences between magistrates' courts and the Crown Court was all that was said to have been given.

Reasons supporting their advice to go to the Crown Court were given by solicitors to all defendants in this group, but the recommendation to 23 defendants to go to the magistrates' court was unsupported in seven cases.

Of the 43 defendants who elected summary trial at a magistrates' court and were later committed to the Crown Court for sentence only 19 per cent said they had talked to a solicitor about the venue for their trial: six were advised to stay and be tried by magistrates, but two of these had not been given any reasons to support the advice.

4.2 Those who acted in accordance with the advice of their solicitor

4.2.1 *Defendants who chose trial at the Crown Court*

Table 15 showed that solicitors had recommended going to the Crown Court for trial to 110 defendants, who eventually followed their advice, and that in 93 cases they gave some explanation to support the advice. In the left-hand column of table 16 is the distribution of reasons said to have been given by the solicitors in support of their advice to choose Crown Court trial, as reported by these 93 defendants. Alongside, for comparison, is given the distribution of reasons for choosing Crown Court trial given by the 100 defendants who, in the earlier question about why they had made such a choice (see table 6), had not mentioned any advice from a solicitor. Thus some of the cases in the left-hand column, are also included in the right-hand column.

Two defendants reported being advised by their solicitor to go to the Crown Court because they would be committed for sentence to a higher court, even if they elected summary trial at a magistrates' court; one defendant was advised to go to the higher court because he had a 'flimsy case', one defendant reported being told that his case was too complicated and involved too many witnesses for the magistrates to deal with, and one defendant said that he had been told that by choosing trial on indictment at the Crown Court a deal could be made between the defence and prosecuting counsel.

Table 16 *Reasons given by solicitors to those defendants who followed their advice and chose to go for trial at the Crown Court, and by those defendants who, in giving their own reasons for choosing Crown Court trial, did not mention 'solicitor's advice'.*

Reasons given for choosing trial at the Crown Court given by	Solicitors 93 = 100%	Defendants 100 = 100%
Base:	%	%
Better chance of being acquitted	37	39
Better chance of a light sentence	14	11
There is a jury to listen to the case	38	56
Can be represented in court	9	11
To find out the evidence for the prosecution	3	2
Time to prepare the case	8	6
Delay of use for some other reason	2	9
Magistrates' court is a 'police court': biased	14	48
The case is gone into more thoroughly: a better hearing	33	73
Judges are better qualified (than magistrates) to hear a case	4	23
Other answers	7	10

These five answers are included in the category of 'other reasons' reported to have been given by solicitors. Also included in this category is the one defendant who reported being told by his solicitor to go to the Crown Court because he would then stand the best chance of a heavy sentence. Both the solicitor and defendant apparently were hoping that during a long term of imprisonment the defendant could be treated for drug addiction.

Of the 93 defendants who were advised by their solicitor to go to the Crown Court for trial, and who followed the advice, 95 per cent thought that all the reasons they had been given by their solicitor in support of the recommendation were good reasons.

It is clear from table 16 that defendants themselves reported many more of their own reasons for going to the Crown Court; fewer reasons were reported to have been given by solicitors. This is unlikely to be a deliberate omission but rather a natural tendency to discuss one's own reasons in somewhat greater detail than those given by someone else; it should however be borne in mind that this may not be the full explanation in support of a solicitor's advice. However, solicitor's reasons, like the defendant's own, were centred around the improved chances of acquittal at the Crown Court. The existence of a jury and the more thorough hearing were the reasons for going to the higher court most frequently mentioned by both solicitors and defendants. Avoiding the magistrates' court because of an alleged bias towards the police by the justices was a reason given by a considerable proportion of defendants who chose trial on indictment at the Crown Court. A significantly smaller proportion of solicitors were reported by defendants to have given this same reason for going to the Crown Court. Bearing in mind that solicitor's reasons have not come direct from the solicitors themselves, but are as reported by the defendants, it would seem nevertheless that some solicitors have misgivings about magistrates' courts in this particular respect.

Defendants themselves were also more likely to want trial at the Crown Court because they thought that it would ensure a more thorough hearing and because the judges are better qualified than magistrates.

It would seem therefore that almost all the arguments put forward for going to the Crown Court by the defendants themselves, are both well founded and reasonable: they follow a pattern which is similar to the reasons said to have been given by solicitors, whose advice would have been based on informed opinion and practice.

4.2.2 *Defendants who elected trial at a magistrates' court, and whose cases were disposed of by the magistrates*

The main reasons solicitors were reported to have given these defendants in support of their own advice to elect summary trial at a magistrates' court were the better chance of a light sentence, the speed with which the case would be dealt, and the cheapness—

the defendant would not be obliged to employ a solicitor and be legally represented. One defendant said that his solicitor had advised going to a magistrates' court because he (the solicitor) could then 'sort it out with the police'.

4.2.3 *Defendants who elected trial at a magistrates' court but who were committed by the magistrates to the Crown Court for sentence*

Two defendants in this group reported being advised by their solicitor to elect summary trial at a magistrates' court in order to have an improved chance of a light sentence. However the main reason reported to have been given by solicitors to this group of defendants was the speed with which the case would be dealt. One defendant reported that he had been advised by his solicitor to stay and be tried by magistrates because the solicitor 'had spoken to the police and had heard their evidence'.

4.2.4 *Summary*

It would appear that although many defendants make a venue decision without the benefit of any professional advice, there is no evidence to show that their decisions are based on very different sorts of reasons from those that qualified legal personnel are reported to have given to their clients in support of their advice. However, it should be remembered that an appreciable proportion of defendants in all three groups had previous convictions recorded against them, and therefore may well have seen a solicitor and taken advice on previous occasions, about which we have no information.

4.3 Those who went against the advice of their solicitor

Only three defendants chose trial on indictment at the Crown Court against the advice of their solicitor, and four defendants, from the group whose cases were disposed of by magistrates chose summary trial at a magistrates' court in preference to going to the Crown Court as advised by their solicitor. The following sections take a special look at these defendants who acted contrary to their solicitor's advice[1].

4.3.1 *Defendants who elected trial at a magistrates' court and whose cases were disposed of by the magistrates: four defendants*

Case 1: The defendant and the solicitor would have preferred trial on indictment at the Crown Court because they thought it involved a better chance of acquittal. However, the defendant was charged with others, and thought that if he went to the Crown Court 'we would all have had to (gone to the Crown Court), and I might have got off, but the others might have got sent down'.

Case 2: The solicitor wanted the case to go to the Crown Court, with a plea of 'not guilty', where he told the defendant he would be acquitted. The defendant however chose summary trial at a magistrates' court and pleaded guilty because he wanted 'to get it done quickly'.

Cases 3 and 4: Husband and wife co-defendants on charges of handling stolen goods. Again, both were advised to go to the Crown Court, plead not guilty, and they would then be acquitted. Both however chose trial at a magistrates' court because they 'wanted to get it over, and didn't want the worry of the case going on'. On the advice of the police they pleaded guilty because, 'they (the police) said we would get fined and could then go home to the baby. He (the solicitor) was furious when we pleaded guilty at the magistrates' court'.

It would appear therefore that particular circumstances forced these four defendants into accepting trial at a magistrates' court, when, under ideal conditions, they would have preferred to have contested the charges at the Crown Court.

4.3.2 *Defendants who chose trial at the Crown Court: three defendants*

Case 1: The solicitor advised summary trial at a magistrates' court and felt the defendant would be convicted and fined. The defendant originally agreed but after three

---

[1] It should be noted that if all defendants had acted in accordance with the advice of their solicitor, by adjusting for the differential sampling fractions used in selecting the three samples from the two levels of court, then the Crown Court would, on balance, have gained more business.

appearances at the magistrates' court when the prosecution witnesses failed to appear, he asked to be committed to the Crown Court. He was subsequently found not guilty of the charges and acquitted.

Cases 2 and 3—apparently unrelated: In both cases the solicitor had recommended summary trial at a magistrates' court without explanation. Both defendants in these cases chose to go to the Crown Court because they believed undue weight would be attached to police evidence at the magistrates' court. Both were convicted by the higher court and sentenced to periods of imprisonment, but neither regretted the choice they had made, and both said they would opt for Crown Court trial again.

One defendant chose summary trial at a magistrates' court and was sentenced by the Crown Court, after being advised to go to the Crown Court for trial by his solicitor. The defendant explained the solicitor's reasons for this advice as follows: 'he (the solicitor) was trying to get me into —— prison hospital for a drinking cure. You have to have two years or over to get into ——, and the magistrate can't give that'. The defendant's own reasons for choosing trial at a magistrates' court however were, 'to get it dealt with there and then', and 'to get less at the magistrates' court than at the Crown Court'. Following conviction at the magistrates' court he was sentenced to 21 months' imprisonment by the Crown Court, and a suspended sentence of three months for a previous conviction was brought into effect, to be served consecutively.

4.4 Advice to defendants from the police as to where to go for trial

4.4.1 *Defendants who chose trial at the Crown Court*

Of the 166 defendants who chose to go for trial at the Crown Court, only 10 per cent reported that the police had, at some stage during their case, told them that they might be able to choose the venue for their trial. Eight of these 17 defendants reported being given advice as to which level of court to choose; the magistrates' court was suggested as a venue to five defendants, and the Crown Court to three defendants. These three defendants who reported being advised by the police to go for trial at the Crown Court had, earlier in the interview, spontaneously mentioned that the advice they had been given by the police was one reason why they had made that particular choice of venue—see table 6, page 12.

4.4.2 *Defendants who elected trial at a magistrates' court and whose cases were disposed of by the magistrates*

Of the 203 defendants who elected summary trial at a magistrates' court and whose cases had been disposed of by the magistrates, 31 per cent reported that the police had at some point during the proceedings for their case, told them that they might be able to choose the venue for their trial. This is a significantly greater proportion of defendants compared with the corresponding group who had chosen to go for trial at the Crown Court.

Of the 65 defendants who were advised of the venue option by the police, 37 per cent reported being told when they were charged, 25 per cent said that they had been told after they had been charged but before their first appearance at the magistrates' court, and the remaining 38 per cent said that the police had only told them about the venue option when they appeared at the magistrates' court.

Of the 65 defendants who reported being told about the venue option by the police, 38 per cent were also advised by them as to which level of court to choose; in every case the advice was to stay at the magistrates' court. Of these 25 defendants, 18 had previously spontaneously mentioned that the advice they had been given by the police was one reason why they had opted for trial at a magistrates' court. Table 7, on page 13, shows that these 18 defendants pleaded guilty to all the charges against them.

4.5 Advice from persons other than a solicitor or the police

Although both the questionnaire and the subsequent analysis attempted to distinguish between the reasons that were reported to have been given by a solicitor or by the police to a defendant in support of a recommendation of a particular venue for trial, and those given by the defendant himself, where a defendant followed the advice given by some other person it is possible that any reasons given to support this advice will have been reported along with the defendant's own reasons and will therefore be included in tables 6, 7, 9 and 11.

4.5.1 Defendants who chose trial at the Crown Court

Of the 166 defendants who chose trial on indictment at the Crown Court, 38 per cent were advised to do so by someone other than a solicitor or the police; 8 per cent were advised to opt for trial at a magistrates' court.

The advice to opt for trial before magistrates was from friends of the defendants—seven cases, from their relatives—five cases, from a co-defendant, and in one case from a court usher. The main sources of advice to opt for trial on indictment at the Crown Court, given to 63 defendants, were friends, 63 per cent, and relatives, 54 per cent. In 3 per cent of cases the advice came from the defendant's employer, and in a similar number of cases from co-defendants. Other sources included probation officers and a legal aid officer.

Although a considerable number of defendants appear to have been given advice as to which venue to choose for their trial, of the 166 defendants who actually chose Crown Court trial, only 2 per cent mentioned that the advice they had been given by someone other than a solicitor or the police, was one reason why they had made such a choice.

4.5.2 Defendants who elected trial at a magistrates' court and whose cases were disposed of by the magistrates

Of the 203 defendants who elected trial before magistrates and whose cases were finally disposed of by the lower court, 10 per cent had been advised to opt for summary trial at a magistrates' court by someone other than a solicitor or the police. This advice came from relatives of the defendant—seven cases, from their friends—11 cases, from their employers—two cases and from a probation officer and a charity information service.

A further 6 per cent had been advised to go to the Crown Court for their trial. This suggestion generally came from friends of the defendants—10 cases, but also from their relatives—two cases, from an usher in court, and from a defendant in another case.

Earlier in the interview when all 203 defendants in this group were asked why they had chosen summary trial at a magistrates' court, only 2 per cent spontaneously mentioned that they had done so because someone, other than a solicitor or the police, had advised that course of action.

That both this proportion, and the comparable figure for those who chose trial at the Crown Court, are so small, may indicate the comparatively minor influence these sources of advice had on a defendant's venue decision.

So far this section has considered both the sources and the nature of the advice given to defendants concerning their venue decision. It has been seen that among defendants who chose to go to the Crown Court the major source of advice was a solicitor, while in contrast those who chose the magistrates' court for their trial were less likely to consult a solicitor, but were more often advised on a course of action by the police. The following section looks at the professional legal support those defendants who chose summary trial at a magistrates' court had when they appeared at court, and in particular examines the reasons why some defendants remained unrepresented throughout their hearing.[1]

4.6 Legal representation at the magistrates' court for defendants who elected summary trial and whose cases were disposed of by the magistrates

Of the 203 defendants who chose to appear before magistrates and whose cases were finally disposed of by the lower court, as many as 64 per cent were not legally represented during the hearing of their case. However of the 13 defendants who pleaded not guilty to all of the charges against them, only two were unrepresented. It was not surprising therefore to find that many defendants said they were not represented because they were pleading guilty and there was no point.

Included in the category of 'other answers' are comments made by three defendants who said that they had engaged solicitors but they had failed to appear at the hearing.

---

[1]Almost all defendants who choose to go for trial at the Crown Court are represented throughout their hearing there.

Table 17 *Reasons for not being represented throughout their case given by defendants who chose trial at a magistrates' court and whose cases were disposed of by the magistrates; those who pleaded guilty to all the charges against them, and those who pleaded not guilty to some or all charges*

Reasons for not being represented during the hearing of the case at a magistrates' court	Defendant pleaded		All who chose trial at a magistrates' court and were unrepresented
	Guilty to all charges	Not guilty to some/all charges	
	%	Nos	%
Was pleading guilty/was guilty—no point	61	(2)*	58
Could manage on my own	44	(4)	44
No time/opportunities to find a solicitor	11	—	10
Could not afford it, too expensive	20	(5)	22
Did not know it was possible	4	(1)	4
Other answers	20	(3)	21
Number on which percentage based[1, 2]	132 = 100%	9 = 100%	141 = 100%

() Denotes number not percentage.
[1] Excludes those not answering.
[2] Percentages add to more than 100, as more than one reason was given by some defendants.
* Defendant A was charged with driving with an excess of alcohol in his blood—S.9 RTA 1972—and with two associated summary offences. He pleaded not guilty to only some charges and explained, 'it was a positive reading . . . but there were extenuating circumstances'. Defendant B was similarly charged, also pleaded not guilty to only some charges, but gave no explanation of his answer to this question.

A further three defendants said that they had approached solicitors who had been unwilling to take on the case; these answers are also included in the group of 'other answers'.

It is interesting to find that 22 per cent of defendants who had chosen summary trial at a magistrates' court and had been unrepresented reported that they had not been represented for reasons of expense. Indeed, this reason, together with that given by the 10 per cent of defendants who said that they had no time to find a solicitor, and the 4 per cent of defendants who reported not knowing it was possible to be represented at a magistrates' court, seems to indicate that about one-third of these defendants who were not represented had inadequate information about the legal aid system.

4.6.1 *The expense of representation*

The expense of representation also appeared to affect the choice of venue a defendant made for his trial: table 7 showed that of the 203 defendants who chose trial at a magistrates' court and whose cases were disposed of by the magistrates, 10 per cent spontaneously mentioned that they had done so because, among other reasons, they felt it would be less expensive than going to the Crown Court. Further investigation of answers given by these 21 defendants showed that 13 were specifically concerned with the expense of obtaining legal representation, and eight defendants were concerned with paying 'costs' to the court as part of the judgment.

The 13 defendants who were concerned with the expense involved in employing a solicitor represent 6 per cent of the total of 203 defendants who chose summary trial at a magistrates' court and whose cases were disposed of by the lower court. All 13 pleaded guilty to all charges. Their answers included the following remarks:

> 'The A.A. (Automobile Association) said it would cost more at the sessions—a solicitor and that'
> '. . . the prohibitive cost of legal representation'
> '. . . the other factor was that it would cut down on expense—the expense of solicitors. People should be able to have a solicitor without having to pay exorbitant amounts of money.'
> 'It means more expense—you have to have a solicitor—it is alright if you have money to spare.'

31

It was interesting to find that as many as 12 of these 13 defendants had been charged with 'drinking and driving' type offences (including failing to provide a specimen of breath or urine); the remaining defendant was charged with theft. Nine of these defendants had previously been found guilty of some offence, including one defendant who had also previously served a custodial sentence.

It would appear therefore that the possible expense involved in getting legal representation not only dissuades some defendants from being represented in court but also discourages some from choosing to go to the Crown Court, although it must be remembered that all 13 defendants in this category were pleading guilty, and it has already been shown that plea is closely related to choice of venue. Nevertheless there are indications that some defendants are not fully aware that they might be eligible for some financial assistance towards the cost of legal representation. General knowledge of, and attitudes towards the legal aid system were not investigated in this study, and therefore it is not known whether *any* contribution by the defendant towards the expense of representation would act as a deterrent to choosing Crown Court trial for some defendants.

5 Defendants' previous experience of the courts and their knowledge of the venue option

The following section looks at the experience defendants had of the two levels of court, both as defendants in previous cases, and in other capacities—such as witnesses, or even spectators. Any familiarity a defendant had with the court system might help him in his venue decision, even if only to make the proceedings seem less overwhelming, and defendants who have records of previous convictions against them are probably able to draw on their previous experiences when making the choice of court for their trial. Indeed it has already been shown that defendants with previous convictions make a choice of·venue for reasons somewhat different from defendants who have never been convicted of any other offence, and attention has previously been drawn to the fact that some 'previous offenders' may never have appeared at court before as a defendant, and similarly that defendants who report having no previous convictions may have previously been charged with offences, appeared at court, and found not guilty and discharged.[1] However, some defendants had had previous experience of the courts other than as defendants in cases themselves, such as appearing as a witness or as a member of a jury and it is this experience that first is discussed below.

5.1.1 Previous experience of the courts other than as a defendant

Table 18 shows the proportions of defendants in each of the three groups who chose the venue for their trial and who had previously been to court in a capacity other than as a defendant.

The experience of the courts other than as a defendant is as the table shows varied.

Table 18 *Proportions of defendants in each of the three groups who chose the venue for their trial, and who had previous experience of some type of court in various other capacities*

Defendants who had been to court on previous occasions	Venue for trial chosen by defendant		
	Crown Court	Magistrates' court	
	Disposal at		
	Crown Court	Magistrates' court	Crown Court
	%	%	%
As a member of a jury	3	6	—
As a plaintiff	9	5	9
As a witness	26	19	26
As a spectator	38	30	46
In some other capacity: but *not* as a defendant	10	8	9
In any of the above capacities	58	47	63
In any of the above capacities, *or* as a defendant	87	77	100
All defendants who chose the venue for their trial: base	166 = 100%	203 = 100%	43 = 100%

[1] See footnote 1 to p 17.

Defendants in all three groups had little experience of the courts either as members of a jury or as complainants, bringing a case against some other person. This is not unexpected; the experience of the defendants in these areas is probably not markedly different from that of non-offenders. However the proportions who had appeared as witnesses—26 per cent, 19 per cent and 26 per cent in the three groups respectively, is probably higher than for people who have never been to court as a defendant; offenders would appear to 'encounter' crime more frequently than non-offenders—even though they may not always be responsible for the offence themselves. This may also account for what seem to be the quite high proportions of defendants, 30 per cent or more in each of the three groups, who have been to court just to watch what went on: the possible explanation being to accompany friends or relatives who were appearing in cases themselves.

5.1.2 Previous experience of the courts as a defendant

Table 19 shows the proportions of defendants in each of the three sample groups who chose the venue for their trial and who had previous convictions recorded against them.

It was noted previously[1] that among the group who had chosen summary trial, and

Table 19 *Proportions of defendants with previous convictions who chose the venue for their trial*

Previous record	Venue for trial chosen by defendant		
	Crown Court	Magistrates' court	
	Disposal at		
	Crown Court	Magistrates' court	Crown Court
	%	%	%
No previous convictions	22	38	2
Previous convictions with:			
a custodial sentence	42	22	82
no custodial sentence	36	40	16
All defendants who chose the venue for their trial: base	166 = 100%	203 = 100%	43 = 100%
Proportions of defendants who had previously appeared at a Crown Court as a defendant	37%	10%	42%

had been sent to the Crown Court for sentence, all but one defendant reported having previous convictions recorded against them, and it was remarked that such a high proportion of previous offenders among this group was not unexpected, since committal for sentence usually requires a defendant to have a record. However the high proportions of defendants in the other two sample groups who also reported being previous offenders was rather surprising. Of the 166 defendants who chose Crown Court trial as many as 78 per cent reported that they had been previously found guilty of some offence, and even among those choosing summary trial at a magistrates' court and whose cases were disposed of at the lower court, 62 per cent said that they had previous convictions recorded against them. This is however a significantly smaller proportion of previous offenders than in either of the other two groups who went to the Crown Court for trial or for sentence only.

Defendants who had been previously convicted of some offence were also asked whether they had ever previously served a custodial sentence in a prison, borstal or

[1] Section 3.3, p 17.

similar penal institution. The proportions of defendants who reported having served custodial sentences on a previous occasion also showed differences between the three sample groups. The smallest proportion was among those whose cases had been disposed of by magistrates, and the greatest proportion who had served previous custodial sentences was from the group who after choosing summary trial at a magistrates' court had been committed for sentence to the Crown Court.

5.1.3 *Summary*

Over half the defendants in each group who chose the venue for their trial had their own previous experience as defendants to help them in making their venue decision. Of the 166 defendants who chose to go before a judge and jury 37 per cent had previously experienced the higher level of court as a defendant, and were presumably sufficiently satisfied to repeat their appearance, and 22 per cent were trying the Crown Court with no previous convictions behind them. At the magistrates' court 38 per cent of those choosing trial at the lower court were making a decision without ever having been previously convicted; and 10 per cent were rejecting trial on indictment at the Crown Court which they had already experienced, in favour of trial before magistrates. Only 13 per cent of those who chose to go to the Crown Court for trial and 23 per cent of those who chose to stay at the magistrates' court were inside a court for the first time.

5.2 Knowing about the venue option

Of the 166 defendants who chose to be tried before a judge and jury, 73 per cent knew that they might be given the chance to say where they wanted their case to be heard even before they were asked to do so at the magistrates' court.

Of the 203 defendants who chose summary trial and whose cases were disposed of at the lower court 65 per cent knew before being told that they might be able to go to the Crown Court if they so wished. Of the 43 defendants choosing summary trial at a magistrates' court and then committed for sentence to the Crown Court 77 per cent knew of the possibility of having a personal choice of venue.

Table 20 shows that the source of this knowledge varied considerably for the three

Table 20 *How defendants learnt about the possibility of being able to choose the venue for their trial*

Defendant knew about the 'option' from	Venue for trial chosen by defendant		
	Crown Court	Magistrates' court	
	Disposal at		
	Crown Court	Magistrates' court	Crown Court
	%	%	%
Previous appearances as a defendant	59	52	88
Watching earlier cases	12	9	15
Other attendances at court	14	18	27
The police	8	34	18
A solicitor	67	19	3
Someone else: probation officer, friend	11	7	12
General knowledge: television, books	7	10	6
Other answers: including from own legal or police training	2	5	—
All defendants who chose venue for their trial and knew about the 'option': base[1]	122 = 100%	133 = 100%	33 = 100%

[1] Percentages add to more than 100 as defendant may have learnt about 'the option' from more than one source.

groups of defendants. The parts played by the police and solicitors are particularly interesting: a much greater proportion of those defendants who chose summary trial at a magistrates' court and whose cases were disposed of at the lower court learnt of the possibility of determining the venue for their trial themselves from the police than did defendants choosing trial on indictment at the Crown Court. The situation was completely reversed with regard to solicitors: those choosing trial at the Crown Court being more likely to have learnt about the 'option' from solicitors than those electing to go to a magistrates' court for their trial. It has already been noted that defendants who chose to go to the Crown Court for trial consulted solicitors about the venue for their trial more often than those who opted for trial before a magistrates' court and this additional information would seem to indicate that solicitors are consulted at a very early stage by those destined for Crown Court trial and that they have an informative as well as an advisory role.

Considerable proportions of all three groups of defendants were aware of the possibility of being able to choose the venue for their trial from their own previous experiences as defendants. This would seem to indicate that previous offences were of a type similar to those currently under consideration, in that they also carried an option as to the venue for the defendant: this therefore may not have been the first occasion on which these defendants had been asked to decide where their case should be heard.

6   Defendants' knowledge of the two court systems

Chapter 5 considered the previous experience defendants had of the two levels of court both as defendants in earlier cases and in various other capacities. From such experience it is thought that some defendants might have learnt or at least have gained impressions about the different levels of court, and in this chapter the knowledge a defendant had of the two levels of court is considered. Such knowledge would have been at a defendant's disposal when he made his choice of venue for trial, and the more knowledge a defendant had in this respect the more likely was his choice to have been a reasoned one.

An informant's knowledge on a particular topic may generally be assessed by one of two methods. One technique is to ask an 'open question', such as 'can you tell me all that you know about . . . ?' probing the reply to ensure that a full answer has been given. This method usually produces lengthy answers each taking a different form and has the disadvantage that classifying the answers is often very time-consuming. An alternative technique is to ask an informant whether he knows about various aspects of the topic under consideration which are put to him in a series of statements. The main drawback of this method is the possibility that an informant might report knowing about every aspect that sounds reasonable when it is put to him.

The timetable imposed on this study severely restricted the use of 'open questions', so an attempt was made to assess and compare the knowledge the various groups of defendants had of the two types of court, by using prompted statements which dealt with various aspects of trial at a magistrates' court and at a Crown Court. In the discussion that follows the limitations of the technique used should be remembered.

6.1 Knowledge of the broad differences between trial at a magistrates' court and trial at the Crown Court

When defendants were asked their reasons for making a particular choice of venue for their trial, many answers included references to what would generally be considered as 'disadvantages' of the 'other' court. In particular the delays associated with Crown Court trial were mentioned by those opting for summary trial at magistrates' courts. However, from the answers to this question it was not possible to assess how much a defendant knew about the 'other' court. Defendants were therefore asked whether they knew about various aspects of trial at the alternative court, and, if not, whether prior knowledge would have led to a change in their venue decision. The aspects asked about were those that would generally be regarded as advantages, and the two tables overleaf show the proportions of defendants who reported knowing about each of the individual aspects of trial at the alternative court at the time they had made their venue decision.

Defendants who chose to go to the Crown Court for trial (table 21) appeared to be generally well aware of the possible attractions of trial at a magistrates' court, especially those aspects concerned with the lack of delay. This would reinforce the earlier view that for defendants such as these the inconveniences of time and money are put aside, their priority was a 'fair' trial with a thorough hearing and the best chance of acquittal; this clearly relates to the fact that 85 per cent of these defendants chose to go for trial at the Crown Court with the intention of pleading not guilty to all the charges against them.

The table indicates that one-third of defendants reported not knowing that a lighter sentence might be imposed by a magistrates' court. Whether this is a true measure of inadequate knowledge or an expression of disbelief in that particular statement is open to question, but knowledge of a magistrates' sentencing powers is discussed later in section 6.2.1 on page 40.

Table 21 *Proportions of defendants who reported knowing about various aspects of summary trial at a magistrates' court: those who chose Crown Court trial before a judge and jury*

Aspects of trial at a magistrates' court	Proportion of defendants reporting knowing about this aspect	Base[1] = all defendants who chose Crown Court trial = 100%
	%	
The case is heard very quickly, there is no delay	86	(161)
Do not have to be represented, so it could be cheaper	72	(162)
If found guilty, might get a lighter sentence from a magistrate	66	(158)
The trial is over quickly, it does not last long	88	(162)
Not likely to be held in custody or on bail for a long time waiting for the case to come up	68	(159)

Table 22 *Proportions of defendants who reported knowing about various aspects of Crown Court trial: those who elected to be tried at a magistrates' court*

Aspects of trial at the Crown Court	Venue for trial chosen by defendant: magistrates' court			
	Disposal at			
	Magistrates' court		Crown Court	
	Proportion reporting knowing about this aspect	Base[1] = all who chose trial at a magistrates' court =100%	Proportion reporting knowing about this aspect	Base[1] = all who chose trial at a magistrates' court =100%
	%		%	
There would be a jury to listen to the case	79	(201)	80	(40)
It is usual to have a qualified person, like a lawyer, to represent the accused	78	(201)	93	(40)
There is likely to be a long wait before the case comes up	65	(201)	95	(40)
Can find out the evidence for the prosecution before even going to court	35	(199)	55	(40)
The case is always heard by someone who has a lot of legal training and experience	67	(201)	85	(40)

[1] Excludes those not answering to a particular item at this question.

Table 22 shows that the two groups of defendants who chose to be tried before magistrates seem to be only marginally less well-informed than their counterparts at the Crown Court centres. One would expect those defendants electing trial at the magistrates' courts to be rather less aware of procedure at the different levels of court, since the proportion of previous offenders is smallest amongst the group whose cases were tried and disposed of at the magistrates' court, and whereas all previous offenders choosing Crown Court trial must have previously appeared at a magistrates' court if only for committal proceedings, there was very little experience of the Crown Court by those whose cases were tried and disposed of at magistrates' courts.

It could be argued that if a defendant is not going to contest the charges laid against him then the fact that another court will provide legal representation, a qualified judge, and a jury, to listen to the case is of little consequence. Since the overwhelming majority of defendants who chose summary trial at a magistrates' court pleaded guilty to all the charges against them, it could therefore be regarded as consistent that while knowing of the 'advantages' associated with trial at the Crown Court they should have nevertheless elected summary trial before magistrates.

It was rather surprising to find that over one-third of defendants who chose trial at a magistrates' court and whose cases were disposed of by the magistrates reported knowing that it was possible to have notice of the evidence for the prosecution before appearing for trial at the Crown Court. This was however the least known aspect of Crown Court trial, as had been expected.

Tables 23 and 24 show how many defendants would have made a different venue decision had their knowledge of a particular facet of trial at the alternative court been better, which is possibly the aspect of this question most relevant to the problem under consideration.

It is apparent from these tables that very few defendants would have changed their venue decisions had they been better informed.

Finding out the case for the prosecution was likely to attract the greatest proportion of defendants to the Crown Court, while the improved chances of avoiding remand at the magistrates' court was the aspect likely to persuade the greatest numbers of those who chose trial at the Crown Court to stay at the lower court. That so few defendants would change their decision with this increased knowledge confirms an earlier impression: when pleading guilty there is little to be gained either from being represented, having a qualified judge and a jury to listen to the case, or even from finding out the case for the prosecution. If, however, the charges are to be contested, then lack of delay is not a pertinent consideration and even though it may involve expense, representation is generally necessary and likely to be advantageous.

Some defendants reported that they would have changed their venue decision had they known about several of the prompted aspects of trial at the alternative court; others said that while some aspects would have prompted them to make a different choice, others would not have led to a change in decision.

Table 23 *Proportions of defendants who would have chosen trial at a magistrates' court had they been better informed on particular aspects of trial at the lower court: those whose cases were tried and disposed of at the Crown Court (numbers and percentages)*

	Aspects of trial at a magistrates' court									
	The trial is over quickly		The case is heard quickly		It is not necessary to be represented		Not likely to be remanded		May get a lighter sentence	
	Nos	%	Nos	%	Nos	%	Nos	%	Nos	%
Defendants not knowing about this aspect of trial at a magistrate's court	20	12	23	14	45	28	51	32	54	34
Of whom would have changed their venue decision, and chosen magistrates' court for trial	4	2	6	4	5	3	11	7	9	6
All defendants who chose Crown Court trial[1]	162	100	161	100	162	100	159	100	159	100

[1] Base: excludes those not answering whether that particular aspect of trial at a magistrates' court was known to them.

Of the 166 defendants who chose trial on indictment at the Crown Court a maximum of 10 per cent would have changed their venue decision and have chosen trial at a magistrates' court for any reason. Of the 203 defendants who chose summary trial at a magistrates' court and whose cases were disposed of at the lower court a maximum of 13 per cent would have changed their decision in favour of the Crown Court. Although the proportions of defendants in these groups who would have made a different venue decision, had their knowledge been better, are not significantly different if account is taken of the differential sampling fractions between the groups then with improved

Table 24 *Proportions of defendants who would have chosen trial at the Crown Court had they been better informed on particular aspects of trial at the high court: those whose cases were tried and disposed of at magistrates' courts (numbers and percentages)[1]*

	Aspects of trial at the Crown Court									
	There is likely to be a long wait before case comes up		It is usual to be represented		Can find out evidence for the prosecution		The case is heard by a qualified judge		There is a jury to listen to the case	
	Nos	%	Nos	%	Nos	%	Nos	%	Nos	%
Defendants not knowing about this aspect of Crown Court trial	71	35	45	22	129	65	67	33	41	20
Of whom would have changed their venue decision, and chosen Crown Court trial	5	2	5	2	20	10	9	4	5	2
All defendants who chose trial at a magistrates' court and whose cases were disposed of by the magistrates: base[2]	201	100	201	100	199	100	201	100	201	100

[1] The corresponding table for those defendants who chose summary trial at a magistrates' court but were committed for sentence to the Crown Court is not given as the numbers involved are too small to draw any meaningful conclusions.

[2] Base: excludes those not answering whether that particular aspect of Crown Court trial was known to them.

knowledge of the differences between the two levels of court more business would pass to the Crown Court.

Towards the end of the interview, defendants were also asked whether, if they could go back and choose again they would still make the same choice of venue for their trial or whether they would choose differently. Not surprisingly at the open question slightly more defendants in all three groups reported wanting to change their decision.[3] For a discussion of the answers to this question and of the reasons given for wanting to make a different decision see section 3.4.

6.2 Detailed knowledge of the various aspects of trial at a magistrates' court and trial at the Crown Court

Having assessed a defendant's knowledge of the more general aspects of trial at the two levels of court, it was then interesting to know whether defendants had any more detailed knowledge of the courts which would have provided a basis for their venue decision.

6.2.1 *The sentencing powers of magistrates*

Some defendants who elected summary trial at a magistrates' court and even some who chose trial at the Crown Court gave as one of their reasons for making such a venue decision the better chance of a light sentence. It was therefore interesting to discover whether defendants knew the maximum penalties that could be imposed by magistrates and also whether those who were particularly concerned with the sentencing aspect of their trial were better informed than defendants who made their choice for other reasons.

Under most circumstances the maximum prison sentence that can be imposed by magistrates for a single offence is six months and the maximum fine £400. Tables 25 and 26 show the numbers of defendants who chose the venue for trial themselves and their estimates of a magistrate's sentencing powers.

Less than a third of those defendants who chose to go for trial to the Crown Court and less than a fifth of those electing summary trial at a magistrates' court whose cases

[3] In answer to this open question of the 166 defendants who chose trial at the Crown Court, 14 per cent reported now wanting trial before magistrates; of the 203 defendants who chose to be tried before magistrates and whose cases were finally disposed of at the lower court, 14 per cent now wanted trial at the Crown Court and, of the 43 defendants who after choosing to be tried at a magistrates' court, were sent to the Crown Court for sentence, 49 per cent now reported wanting trial at the Crown Court.

were disposed of by the magistrates, knew that the maximum prison sentence that could be imposed by the lower court was six months. Those who were tried at the Crown Court were more likely to be correct than those whose cases were disposed of by magistrates, their knowledge presumably coming in part at least from their greater experience of the courts. As expected those defendants whom the magistrates sent to the Crown Court for sentence were most likely to be able to provide the correct answer. Very few of this group would not attempt to provide an answer to this question, while nearly one-quarter of each of the other two groups reported having no idea of the sentencing powers of magistrates.

Although table 25 shows that considerable proportions of defendants in each group overestimated the sentence that could be imposed by magistrates, it gives no indication

Table 25 *Proportions of defendants who overestimated, underestimated and correctly estimated the maximum prison sentence that can be imposed by magistrates: those who chose the venue for their trial*

Defendant's estimate of maximum prison sentence	Venue for trial chosen by defendant		
	Crown Court	Magistrates' court	
	Disposal at		
	Crown Court	Magistrates' court	Crown Court
	%	%	%
Less than six months	1	2	—
Six months	29	19	42
More than six months	47	56	53
Spontaneous: don't know	23	23	5
All defendants who chose the venue for their trial: base[1]	165 = 100%	203 = 100%	43 = 100%

Table 26 *Proportions of defendants who overestimated, underestimated and correctly estimated the maximum fine that can be imposed by magistrates: those who chose the venue for their trial*

Defendant's estimate of maximum fine	Venue for trial chosen by defendant		
	Crown Court	Magistrates' court	
	Disposal at		
	Crown Court	Magistrates' court	Crown Court
	%	%	%
Less than £400	31	38	35
£400	3	1	7
More than £400	15	16	7
No limit	3	2	7
Spontaneous: don't know	48	43	44
All defendants who chose the venue for their trial: base[1]	165 = 100%	203 = 100%	43 = 100%

[1] Excludes those not answering.

of how far out defendants were in the estimates they made: a small margin of error might be regarded as of little consequence. Further analysis showed that of those defendants who estimated that magistrates could impose maximum prison sentences of more than six months, among those who chose to be tried at the Crown Court, and among those who chose to be tried by magistrates but who were committed to the Crown Court for sentence, estimates of a maximum prison sentence of between seven and 12 months were made by over half the defendants in each group. However, similar maximum sentences were estimated by only one-third of the group who chose summary trial and whose cases were tried and disposed of by magistrates, but nearly as many again of this same group estimated maximum prison sentences of four years or longer. Less than 10 per cent of either of the other two groups made estimates this far removed from the actual maximum of six months.

It is interesting to note that among all three groups the general tendency was to over-estimate the maximum prison sentence that could be imposed, whereas as can be seen from table 26 the tendency was reversed with respect to the maximum fine; of those defendants who were prepared to attempt an estimate, the majority underestimated the maximum fine that could be imposed by magistrates. Even fewer defendants in all three groups were prepared to estimate the maximum fine than had attempted to say what the maximum prison sentence was, and still fewer were correct in their estimate.

Of those who made incorrect estimates of the maximum fine that could be imposed by magistrates, further analysis showed that over two-thirds of each group estimated that the maximum fine was less than £250; this includes about 10 per cent of each group who put the figure as low as less than £100. Less than 10 per cent of defendants in any group made an estimate either in the range of £250 to £399, or in the range £401 to less than £500—reasonable errors on the actual maximum of £400. However about 20 per cent of each group estimated a maximum fine of £500, and the remaining defendants put the figure at £1,000 or even higher.

It would be expected that defendants who mentioned the improved chances of a light sentence as a reason to support the choice of venue they made would be more likely than those not especially concerned with that aspect of their trial to know the maximum fine that could be imposed at a magistrates' court. However, analysis showed that those defendants who made a particular choice of venue because of the better chance of a light sentence were no more likely to be correct in their estimate of the maximum fine and the maximum prison sentence than defendants who did not mention this aspect of their trial.

It is suggested therefore that defendants in all three groups were generally ill-informed as regards the sentencing powers of magistrates, and although a proportion of defendants gave what was a valid reason for going to the magistrates' court—that they would stand a better chance of a light sentence—they personally had little accurate knowledge to support their reasoning.

6.2.2 At what stage of a trial is a defendant's record (if any) made known?

A defendant's record is only made known to a magistrate after the verdict has been decided upon, but before sentence is passed. At the Crown Court the details of a defendant's record are included in the documents relating to the case which are before the judge throughout the hearing. However, it is a matter for the judge's own discretion to decide whether or not to inquire if the defendant has any previous convictions by looking through these documents. In any case a defendant's record will never be made known to the jury until after they have reached their verdict.

An appreciable number of defendants in all three groups were concerned with what they saw as unfairness and bias at a particular type of court, and answers occasionally indicated that particular courts were avoided by defendants because, among other reasons, they 'were known'. It has already been noted that over 60 per cent of defendants in each of the three groups who chose the venue for their trial had previously been found guilty of some other offence—possibly very minor and it is of course possible that regular offenders had appeared before the same magistrate on more than one occasion and that they might have been recognised. Equally of course defendants who had previously been to court but who had been acquitted and were hence not recorded as 'previous offenders', might have appeared before the same magistrates on other occasions and might have been recognised.[1] However, it was of interest to know whether defendants knew that, officially, any record of previous convictions could only be revealed at a specified point in the trial. Several defendants did spontaneously mention that while their record was supposed to be revealed only after conviction at a magistrates' court, they believed that the police could put this knowledge across to the bench in the way they presented their evidence without making a formal statement as such; they believed that in this respect practice and theory were very different.

Tables 27 and 28 show the various stages of the trial at which defendants thought a man's record would be made known firstly to a magistrate, and then to a Crown Court judge.

Table 27 *Knowledge of when a magistrate is told of a defendant's previous convictions, by those defendants who chose the venue for their trial*

Magistrate is told of previous convictions	Venue for trial chosen by defendant		
	Crown Court	Magistrates' court	
	Disposal at		
	Crown Court	Magistrates' court	Crown Court
	%	%	%
Before hearing any evidence	25	28	32
After hearing the evidence, but before conviction	17	34	32
After conviction	41	24	32
Not at all	2	1	2
Spontaneous: no idea	15	12	2
All defendants who chose the venue for their trial: base[2]	162 = 100%	201 = 100%	41 = 100%

Table 28 *Knowledge of when a Crown Court judge is told of a defendant's previous convictions, by those defendants who chose the venue for their trial*

Crown Court judge is told of previous convictions	Venue for trial chosen by defendant		
	Crown Court	Magistrates' court	
	Disposal at		
	Crown Court	Magistrates' court	Crown Court
	%	%	%
Before hearing any evidence	29	24	33
After hearing the evidence but before the jury has reached a verdict	16	16	26
After the jury has reached a verdict	41	22	33
Not at all	2	1	5
Spontaneous: no idea	12	36	2
All defendants who chose the venue for their trial: base[2]	164 = 100%	203 = 100%	42 = 100%

[1] See footnote 1 to p 17.
[2] Excludes those not answering.

43

The data shown in these two tables must be treated with caution for the following two reasons. Firstly, because the range of possible answers to the questions were put to the defendants; their answers were not given unprompted. This means that the number of defendants who are recorded as having given the correct answer may be slightly larger than the number who would have given the same answer to an unprompted question. The tables may also include some defendants who chose the correct answer because it seemed to be the most reasonable, and even some who made a completely random choice from the range of answers provided. Secondly, at the Crown Court the situation with regard to the declaration of previous convictions is not as clearly defined as at the lower courts: there may have been some confusion by respondents between the stage at which the judge can find out about a man's record if he wishes to do so, and the later stage, when the record may be declared to the jury in open court.

Bearing these two points in mind the tables nevertheless show several points of interest.

Comparatively small proportions of all three groups, despite their own previous experience, correctly identified the stage of the trial at either level of court when previous convictions are made known to the presiding justice. More disquieting is the fact that over half the defendants in each of the two groups who chose trial at a magistrates' court and more than a third of those who chose trial on indictment at the Crown Court thought that any record was revealed to a magistrate at what would probably be a most prejudicial stage of the trial; before a verdict is reached. A greater proportion of those who chose Crown Court trial than of those who chose to be tried before magistrates and whose cases were disposed of at the lower court were able to provide the correct answer; this is partly accounted for by the greater proportion of defendants among the former group who had been previously convicted of some offence and had served a custodial sentence.

As regards Crown Court trial, there were no appreciable differences between the three groups in the proportions who reported correctly the point in court proceedings when a judge had information concerning a man's record. Of the 166 defendants who chose to be tried at the Crown Court, 41 per cent reported that previous convictions were made known to the judge only after the jury had reached a verdict. Since the majority of defendants tried at the Crown Court had previous convictions (78 per cent) which had probably been declared, it seems probable as was suggested earlier that some defendants confused the point at which the judge had the information before him concerning a man's record and the point at which it could be declared in open court to a jury.

Despite the inadequacies of this data, there would seem to be indications that not only are there appreciable numbers of defendants who genuinely do not know about this aspect of court procedure, but there are also considerable numbers who believe that previous records are brought up at the magistrates' court at a time which would prejudice the outcome of any trial. This belief may well account for, or reinforce, any existing prejudice which defendants already have against the fairness of magistrates' courts.

6.2.3 *The differences between a stipendiary magistrate and a lay magistrate*

A stipendiary magistrate was identified to a defendant as a justice who could hear a case on his own; lay magistrates they were told had to hear cases together, usually in threes. Defendants were then asked whether they knew of any other differences between stipendiary and lay magistrates.

The majority of defendants in each of the three groups who chose the venue for their trial reported not knowing of any other differences between a stipendiary magistrate and lay magistrates. Only 13 per cent of the 166 defendants who had chosen to go for trial to the Crown Court, only 7 per cent of the 203 defendants who had chosen to be tried at a magistrates' court and whose cases were disposed of by the magistrates, and only 16 per cent of the 43 defendants who after electing to be tried by magistrates had been sent to the Crown Court for sentence could give one correct difference between a stipendiary magistrate and a lay magistrate. The distinction most frequently mentioned by all three groups of defendants was the professional training and qualifications of the stipendiary magistrate. Very few defendants mentioned that a stipendiary magistrate is a full-time justice, or that he receives a salary. There were a few more defendants in each of the three groups who chose the venue for their trial who said that they knew of differences between stipendiary magistrates and lay magistrates, but they then gave what were quite incorrect differences. The most common misconception was that a stipendiary magistrate could impose a longer or heavier sentence than a lay magistrate. One defendant however thought that 'the one on his own doesn't know enough about the law to sentence people to prison' and one defendant was under the impression that lay magistrates dealt with 'domestic cases, divorces and domestic squabbles, not really criminal cases'.

6.2.4 *Appearances at the magistrates' court before stipendiary and lay magistrates*

It has previously been shown that the majority of defendants in each of the three groups who chose the venue for their trial were unaware of the differences between stipendiary and lay magistrates. It is therefore unlikely that defendants whose initial appearance at court was before a lay magistrate were more likely than defendants who initially appeared before stipendiary magistrates to have chosen to go to the Crown Court for trial: the choice of venue and the reasons given for making that choice have already been shown to be closely related to the plea a defendant intends making in answer to the charges against him. Defendants who chose Crown Court trial reported doing so because they wanted a more thorough hearing of their case, a jury to listen to their case, and what they saw as the best chance of acquittal. Nevertheless, if defendants who initially appeared before lay magistrates were more likely to have chosen to go to the Crown Court for trial then of all defendants who chose Crown Court trial the proportion who had initially appeared before lay magistrates would be expected to be significantly greater than the proportion of defendants who had appeared before lay magistrates among all those who chose summary trial at a magistrates' court.

Table 29 *Proportions of defendants (reporting) appearing before lay magistrates at the time they made their venue decision: those who chose the venue for their trial[1]*

	Venue for trial chosen by defendant	
	Crown Court	Magistrates' court
	Disposal at	
	Crown Court	Magistrates' court
	%	%
Defendants (reporting) appearing before lay magistrates	66	66
Defendants (reporting) appearing before stipendiary magistrates	34	34
All defendants who chose the venue for their trial: base	166 = 100%	203 = 100%

[1] For defendants who elected summary trial at a magistrates' court the information was taken from court records at the time of sampling. For defendants who chose Crown Court trial this information was taken from the interview questionnaires.

The table shows that of those defendants who chose Crown Court trial the proportion who initially appeared before lay magistrates is equal to the proportion of defendants who initially appeared before stipendiary magistrates among those who chose summary trial at a magistrates' court and whose cases were disposed of by the magistrates. There is therefore no evidence to show that defendants who initially appear before lay magistrates are more likely to choose Crown Court trial than those whose appearance at the magistrates' court is before a stipendiary magistrate.

6.3 Conclusions

It has been shown that, in general, defendants were aware of the main differences between the two court systems, and of the possible advantages associated with them, but that not surprisingly, they were not particularly well-informed on the more detailed points, such as the sentencing powers of the magistrates. It has also previously been suggested that the reasons given by defendants for making a particular choice are realistic, and consistent with the plea they enter (see section 3.2) and by taking the reasons together with the plea into account, it is possible to explain why some of the so-called advantages of each type of court were not valid considerations to a defendant when he made his choice of venue.

However, before asking about their knowledge of the two court systems, defendants had been asked whether they, personally, felt that at the time they had been asked to decide where to have their case heard, they knew enough about magistrates' courts and the Crown Court to be able to make such a choice. Of the 166 defendants who chose Crown Court trial, 46 per cent felt that at the time they had made their choice of venue for their trial they did not know enough about the two types of court. A similar proportion of those defendants who after choosing to be tried by magistrates had been sent to the Crown Court for sentence also felt their knowledge to be inadequate in this respect. However, of the 203 defendants who chose to be tried at a magistrates' court and whose cases were disposed of by the magistrates, 60 per cent, a significantly greater proportion compared with those who chose Crown Court trial, thought they did not know enough about the two levels of court.

Despite there being appreciable numbers of defendants in all three groups who felt that they did not have sufficient knowledge to help them in coming to a venue decision, it seems that while the choice of venue, the plea and the reasons to support the choice remain so closely related, providing defendants with more detailed information about the two levels of court is unlikely to persuade large numbers of defendants who would otherwise choose trial at the Crown Court, to consent to trial at a magistrates' court.

7 The importance to the defendant of being able to choose the venue for trial

7.1 Those who reported choosing the venue for their trial

Having discussed with defendants their reasons for making a particular choice of venue for their trial, they were then asked to assess, on a four point scale, the importance at the time of being able to choose where to have their case heard. Table 30 shows the importance of the venue option to each of the three groups of defendants who chose the venue for their own trial.

Table 30 *Proportions of defendants who, at the time they made their venue decision, thought that being given an option of where to go for trial was important*

Being given an option of venue was	Venue for trial chosen by defendant		
	Crown Court	Magistrates' court	
	Disposal at		
	Crown Court	Magistrates' court	Crown Court
	%	%	%
Very important	70	29	29
Important	19	22	22
Not very important	5	24	22
Not important at all	6	34	27
All defendants who chose the venue for their trial: base[1]	163 = 100%	196 = 100%	41 = 100%

[1] Excludes those not answering.

Being allowed to exercise some choice over where their case should be heard was important to a very much greater proportion of defendants who opted for Crown Court trial than for either those who elected trial at a magistrates' court and whose cases were disposed of by the magistrates, or for those who were committed by magistrates to the Crown Court for sentence. Nearly 90 per cent of those who chose trial at the Crown Court thought that being given a personal choice was to some extent important to them, while less than one-half of those defendants who chose trial before magistrates and whose cases were disposed of at the lower court had similar feelings. There was no evidence to show that in any of the three groups of defendants those who pleaded not guilty to all the charges against them were more likely than those who pleaded guilty to think that the venue option had been either very important or important.

It had previously been found that of the 203 defendants who chose to be tried by magistrates and whose cases were disposed of at the lower court, as many as 53 per cent had indicated that one reason why they had elected summary trial at a magistrates' court was to avoid delay at various stages of their trial.[2] It was subsequently found that of the 114 defendants who chose summary trial, whose cases were disposed of by the magistrates, and who said that being given a choice of venue had been either 'not

[2] See footnote 1 p 15.

very important' or 'not important at all', 41 per cent had supported their statement by saying that it had not mattered where their case was heard, 'as long as it could be dealt with quickly'. In the light of the earlier findings concerning the apparent importance attached to a quick trial, the answers given by this particular group of defendants might be inconsistent.

There remains however a significantly greater proportion of defendants who thought that the option was either 'very important' or 'important' amongst those who chose trial on indictment at the Crown Court than in either of the other two groups who chose the venue for their trial. It should nevertheless be noted that if those who had chosen trial at a magistrates' court had been given no choice of venue, but had instead been tried summarily at the magistrates' court either by statutory procedure, or at the request of the prosecution, it could not be assumed that having no personal choice of venue would then not have mattered; the right to choose *not* to go to the Crown Court, may be as important as the right to choose trial by jury.

Apart from the group discussed above, for whom the venue option had been unimportant as long as their case was dealt with quickly, there remain four main reasons why having the right to choose a venue for trial was not felt to be important given by those who chose to be tried by magistrates and whose cases were disposed of by the magistrates. The most frequently mentioned reason was, not surprisingly, associated with plea: of these 67 defendants nearly 40 per cent gave reasons in the following form:

'I was pleading guilty, so it didn't matter where I was tried'.
'It was not important this time, as I was going to plead guilty'.
'Because we were guilty we had nothing to fight for'.

The inference is clear: had the plea been one of not guilty, choosing the venue for trial would have been important.

About one-third of the same group saw no differences between the two courts as far as the likely outcome was concerned, and so thought it unimportant that they had been given a choice: 'wherever you go the result will be the same', 'it doesn't make any difference to the result, the judgement will be according to the law, wherever you are'. Of these 67 defendants 25 per cent said that as their case was only a minor one it had not been important that they had been allowed to choose where to go for trial, and just over 10 per cent of defendants in this group said that being given the choice was of no importance since they did not know enough about the courts or the differences between them.

It would seem, therefore, that having a personal choice of venue for trial was unimportant to some defendants simply because of the particular circumstances of their case—they were pleading guilty, or it was only a minor charge. Only one-third of this group saw no likely differences in the outcome whichever court they went to and hence were not concerned about being allowed to choose for themselves, but, as was mentioned earlier, it cannot be certain that these particular defendants would have given the same answer had they been pleading 'not guilty'.

The few defendants who chose Crown Court trial, but felt that being allowed to do so was unimportant, said this was because there was never any 'real' choice, mainly because the court had already decided how to deal with their case . . .

'I've been through this before and I just knew that question which court you wanted to be tried at was a farce. They (the magistrates) had already made up their minds before you go which one you're going to'.
'The magistrates would have had to commit me to the Crown Court in the end and could only have listened to me and then sent me to the Crown Court—because I was on a suspended sentence from a Crown Court'.

A few defendants felt there was no 'real' choice because they had to take their solicitor's advice, and one defendant said that as he did not know much about the courts, it was not important that he had been given an option of venue for his trial.

7.2 Those who reported having had no personal choice of venue for their trial

Not all defendants reported being given the option of choosing the venue for their trial themselves, and in Chapter 2 an attempt was made to explain why the venue option may never have been put to some defendants. It was concluded that some defendants had probably chosen the venue for their trial but failed to appreciate doing so, while for the majority it was thought likely that, considering the nature or circumstances of their offence, the venue for their trial had been determined by statutory provision or by the prosecution.

The three groups who reported having been given no choice of venue for their trial were asked whether at the time, this had mattered to them or not.

Their answers to this question are set out in table 31.

Table 31 *Defendants who felt that being given no choice of venue for their trial mattered*

Being given no choice of venue for their trial	Venue for trial		
	Crown Court	Magistrates' court	
	Disposal at		
	Crown Court	Magistrates' court	Crown Court
	%	%	%
Mattered to the defendant	48	13	(2)
Did not matter to the defendant	52	87	(12)
All defendants who reported having been given no choice of venue for their trial: base	96 = 100%	23 = 100%	14

Again there was no evidence that defendants who pleaded not guilty to all the charges against them were more likely than those who pleaded guilty to think that not being given a choice of venue mattered.

However, although the base numbers for two of the three sample groups are small, it is nevertheless clear (and not surprising) that having had no choice of where their case was to be heard was important to a much greater proportion of defendants who were sent to the Crown Court for trial than to those who were tried summarily by magistrates.

Of the 47 defendants who reported being sent for trial to the Crown Court, having been given no personal choice of venue mattered to over three-quarters because they had wanted a quick trial. The remaining answers explaining why it mattered not having been given an option of venue for trial were generally concerned with the wider principles: with personal rights and liberty being at stake.

7.2.1 *Why having been given no choice of venue for trial did not matter to some defendants*

Nine of the 49 defendants sent to the Crown Court for trial, and one defendant who was dealt with summarily by magistrates said that having been given no choice of venue for their trial had not mattered since their cases were heard at the court they would have chosen had they been given the option of doing so. Presumably if the venue had been different, these defendants would have felt more strongly about being denied a personal choice.

Two defendants tried on indictment at the Crown Court and four who were dealt with at the lower courts said that as at the time they did not know much about the courts or the differences between them it had not mattered that they had never been given the option of choosing where to go for trial. A further four defendants from each of these two groups, and one defendant who had been committed from a magistrates' court to the Crown Court for sentence, felt, like some defendants who had been given the choice, that it did not really matter where the case was heard as both courts would come to the same conclusion—there was no difference between them.

The only other reason mentioned by any appreciable proportion of defendants was that given by those who had been sent for trial to the Crown Court; it had not mattered that they had never been given any option because even if they had elected to appear before magistrates they felt that their records would have ensured that they would be sent up for sentence to the Crown Court.

The remaining reasons indicated a general apathy towards the whole question of venue; some defendants seemed unconcerned with where their case was heard:

'I couldn't have cared less where they sent me'.
'Don't know, it just was not important'.
'I've never been to court before, so I didn't really mind what happened'.

7.3 The importance of the venue option for a range of other offences

Although some defendants felt it was important that they had been allowed to say where they wanted to have their case heard, it was also of interest to know whether they felt the same way about a range of other offences. That is, was the right to choose the venue for trial important only because there were particular circumstances surrounding the offence, was it perhaps related to the seriousness of the offence, or is it always important that a defendant should be able to determine the venue for his trial?

To find out the views of defendants on this topic they were asked to say for a range of nine offences firstly how serious they regarded each offence, as measured by a four-point scale, and then whether they thought it important that a defendant charged with that offence should be allowed to say whether he wanted to be tried before magistrates, or before a judge at the Crown Court.[1]

Table 32 shows the proportions of defendants in each of the three groups who chose the venue for their own trial thinking that nine different offences are either 'very serious' or 'serious'. (The proportions not shown in the table—to add to 100 per cent, are those who said the offence is either 'minor' or 'not really an offence at all'.) Table 33 shows the proportions of defendants in each of the same three groups who thought that for each of the nine offences it was important that anyone charged with that offence should be able to choose the venue for his trial.

Table 32 *Proportions of defendants thinking that nine different offences are either very serious or serious: those who chose the venue for their trial*

Offence	Venue for trial chosen by defendant					
	Crown Court		Magistrates' court			
	Disposal at					
	Crown Court		Magistrates' court		Crown Court	
	Offence is serious	Base[2] = 100%	Offence is serious	Base[2] = 100%	Offence is serious	Base[2] = 100%
	%		%		%	
Rape	100	(160)	99	(191)	100	(40)
Burglary	80	(153)	80	(188)	72	(39)
Dangerous driving	84	(153)	88	(180)	82	(40)
Assaulting a policeman	73	(149)	75	(182)	65	(40)
Deliberately damaging property	82	(154)	82	(186)	85	(40)
Drinking and driving	83	(141)	82	(153)	73	(40)
Shoplifting	28	(150)	47	(161)	35	(37)
Travelling on public transport without paying	7	(160)	12	(188)	5	(40)
Not having a television licence	4	(161)	9	(188)	—	(39)

[1] In asking defendants to assess the seriousness of various offences, it was not intended to use the data from that question to 'rank' offences in order of seriousness but only to discover whether there was any relationship between the importance of the accused being able to choose the venue for his trial, and the seriousness of the offences as judged by our informants.
() Denotes number not percentage.
[2] The base numbers in the three groups vary for different offences, and are usually smaller than the total number of defendants who chose the venue for their trial in that group. This is because defendants were not asked to comment on any offence they had been personally charged with on this occasion. Any defendant who could not give an answer, or who was not asked the question by error, is also omitted from the base number.

Table 33 *Proportions of defendants thinking that for nine different offences it is important that a person charged with that offence should be able to choose the venue for trial: those who chose the venue for their own trial*

Offence	Venue for trial chosen by defendant					
	Crown Court				Magistrates' court	
	Disposal at					
	Crown Court		Magistrates' court		Crown Court	
	Choice is important	Base[1] = 100%	Choice is important	Base[1] = 100%	Choice is important	Base[1] = 100%
	%		%		%	
Rape	82	(160)	76	(191)	65	(40)
Burglary	86	(153)	73	(188)	75	(39)
Dangerous driving	81	(153)	77	(180)	82	(40)
Assaulting a policeman	85	(149)	77	(182)	78	(40)
Deliberately damaging property	71	(154)	69	(186)	63	(40)
Drinking and driving	74	(141)	73	(153)	85	(40)
Shoplifting	65	(150)	71	(161)	79	(37)
Travelling on public transport without paying	49	(160)	52	(188)	45	(40)
Not having a television licence	40	(161)	46	(188)	51	(39)

() Denotes number not percentage.
[1] See footnote 2 to table 32.

As can be seen from table 32 the proportions of defendants in each of the three groups who regarded any particular offence as serious were not significantly different, with the exception of the offence of 'shoplifting': a greater proportion of those defendants whose cases had been tried and disposed of by magistrates, than of those who chose to be tried at the Crown Courts thought that 'shoplifting' was a serious offence.

Variation between offences in the proportions of defendants who regarded them as serious is much as expected. The offences are listed in the tables in what was thought to be the order of seriousness that most people would agree upon, and the only surprising result concerned the offence of 'assaulting a policeman'. This was not considered to be a serious offence by rather more defendants than had been anticipated. Spontaneous comments were added to the answers of some defendants who regarded 'assaulting a policeman' as only a 'minor offence' or as 'not really an offence at all' and these suggest that this particular offence was not being considered in a frivolous manner. Such comments included 'they (the police) expect it', 'its what they are paid for—its all part of their job'.

7.3.1 *The importance of the venue option for a range of nine offences*

Under the present system not all of the nine offences that were put to defendants carry a venue option. Cases of 'rape' must always be heard by Crown Court judges, while 'not having a television licence' can only be dealt with summarily by magistrates. Cases of 'assault on a policeman' may be heard either at the Crown Court or a magistrates' court but at present the decision does not rest with the defendant. Table 33 shows that for all nine offences the right of a defendant to choose the venue for trial was thought to be important by considerable proportions of informants in all three sample groups. Even for the comparatively minor offence of 'not having a television licence', 40 per cent or more of defendants in the three sample groups thought it important that the accused should be able to choose where to go for trial.

By relating table 32 to table 33 it can be seen that there is an association between the seriousness of an offence and the importance of the venue option and it had been hoped that it would be possible to see for the whole range of offences whether those defendants who regarded a particular offence as serious were more likely to think the venue option important than those who saw it as only a 'minor' offence or as 'not really an offence at all'.

However, with the exception of the offence of 'shoplifting', there were always too few defendants in one or other of the categories of 'seriousness', to be able to make reliable comparisons. For the offence of 'shoplifting' among defendants who chose to be tried at the Crown Court, and for those who chose summary trial and whose cases were disposed of by magistrates, those who regarded 'shoplifting' as serious were indeed found to be more likely to think a venue option important, than those who regarded this as a less serious offence.

7.4 Conclusions

Considerable proportions of defendants in each of the three sample groups who chose the venue for their own trial thought that for each of nine different offences it was important that the accused should be able to choose the venue for his trial. There also appeared to be a relationship between the seriousness of an offence, as assessed by defendants, and the importance of having a venue option for that offence, but even for the offence of 'not having a television licence', which was regarded as serious by less than 10 per cent of defendants in any group, and which at present can only be dealt with summarily by magistrates, at least one-third of defendants in each group felt that the offence should carry a venue option for the accused.

8 Defendants' attitudes to their trial, its outcome, and their suggestions for improvements

8.1 Defendants' attitudes to their own trial and to the court systems in general

The first part of this section deals with data taken from the answers to a question where a series of statements, purporting to have been made by other persons about going to court, were read to a defendant. The defendant was then asked to indicate his agreement or disagreement with each statement measured on a four-point scale. Defendants who spontaneously said that they neither agreed nor disagreed with a particular statement were recorded as 'neutral'.

This data was not expected to show accurately how each group of defendants felt about their trial: it is probably unrealistic to expect, for example, that any convicted defendant will view his trial in an entirely favourable light. But it was hoped that the data would provide a basis on which the feelings of defendants in each of the three groups who chose the venue for their trial could be compared.

For discussion the statements have been divided into two groups: those expressing favourable attitudes towards the courts, and those making unfavourable comments; on the questionnaire the statements were not separated in this way.

Table 34 shows the proportions of defendants in each of the three sample groups who chose the venue for their trial who said they either agreed strongly or mildly with each of the statements and the proportions who disagreed either strongly or mildly.

8.1.1 Statements which expressed favourable attitudes towards the courts

All three sample groups who chose the venue for their trial contain appreciable proportions of defendants who disagreed with some of these favourable comments.

Considerably more than half of those defendants who had appeared at the Crown Court either for trial or only for sentence (62 per cent and 60 per cent respectively) indicated that they were given insufficient opportunities during their trial to say what they wanted. Those defendants who were tried at the higher courts would have been legally represented, but despite this, it seems that they would like more opportunities to speak for themselves.[1]

The majority of defendants in all three groups agreed that a jury paid as much attention to a defendant's evidence as to police evidence, although not surprisingly a considerable proportion (44 per cent) of those defendants whose cases had been disposed of summarily by magistrates felt 'neither one way or the other'—appearing before a jury was outside their experience on this occasion. However nearly one-quarter of those who chose to appear before a jury for trial at the Crown Court thought that a jury was not invariably impartial, and 72 per cent of this group thought that a defendant did not always get a fair trial.

Over two-thirds of defendants who chose to be tried by magistrates and were sentenced by Crown Court judges and over half of the defendants whose cases were completed at the magistrates' courts also disagreed with the statement 'one always get a fair trial'. Indeed as many as 56 per cent of defendants who were committed for sentence to the Crown Court, 42 per cent of those whose cases were tried and disposed of at magistrates' courts, and 47 per cent of those who chose to be tried at the Crown Court disagreed strongly with this same statement.

Strong disagreement with the statement, 'one is innocent until proved guilty', was also

---

[1] See also 8.4 which discusses improvements to court procedure suggested by the defendants themselves.

Table 34 *Proportions of defendants agreeing/disagreeing[1] with statements expressing favourable and unfavourable attitudes towards the two court systems: those who chose the venue for their trial*

	Venue for trial chosen by defendant								
	Crown Court			Magistrates' court					
	Disposal at								
	Crown Court			Magistrates' court			Crown Court		
	Agree	Dis-agree	Base[2] = 100%	Agree	Dis-agree	Base[2] = 100%	Agree	Dis-agree	Base[2] = 100%
	%	%		%	%		%	%	%
Favourable comments. Some people have said that . . .									
they had all the opportunities they needed to say what they wanted	35	62	(165)	64	35	(203)	40	60	(43)
one always gets a fair trial	24	72	(161)	39	55	(201)	28	70	(43)
the jury paid as much attention to what they said as to what the police said	68	22	(164)	41	15	(194)	51	23	(43)
one is innocent until proved guilty	48	49	(163)	59	36	(201)	45	52	(43)
Unfavourable comments. Some people have said that . . .									
the whole thing was so overwhelming that they didn't always understand what was happening	66	32	(165)	57	39	(203)	66	35	(43)
there were times when they couldn't hear what was being said	61	38	(165)	52	47	(203)	68	32	(43)
the magistrate paid more attention to what the police said than to what they said	81	10	(165)	68	27	(203)	88	11	(43)
the court didn't take sufficient notice of what made them commit the offence	66	16	(162)	61	30	(202)	79	16	(42)
the man who is well-off financially gets a lighter sentence from magistrates than the poor man who commits the same offence	53	33	(165)	51	40	(203)	53	35	(43)

[1] Those defendants who said spontaneously that they neither agreed nor disagreed with the statement —recorded as neutral—have been omitted from the table which explains why the percentages do not add to 100.

[2] Excludes those not answering.

registered by 40 per cent of defendants who chose trial at the Crown Court, by 22 per cent of defendants who chose to be tried by magistrates and whose cases were disposed of at the lower court, and by 38 per cent of defendants who chose to be tried by magistrates but who were sent to the Crown Court for sentence. A greater proportion of defendants who were tried and whose cases were disposed of by magistrates, compared with those who chose to be tried at the Crown Court, said that they agreed with this statement (59 per cent compared with 48 per cent). It must be remembered however that nearly all defendants who chose summary trial at a magistrates' court pleaded guilty and therefore, on this occasion, had not experienced contesting the charges against them: they personally had not tested the statement, 'one is innocent until proved guilty'.

The answers given to these series of statements by those defendants who chose to be tried at the Crown Court and by those who chose trial at a magistrates' court and whose cases were disposed of at the lower court were compared on the basis of the plea that had been made in answer to the charges laid against them.[3] The analysis showed only one significant difference: defendants who chose trial on indictment at the Crown Court and pleaded guilty to some or all the charges against them were more

[3] See tables C11 and C12, appendix C, pp 80 and 81.

likely than those who pleaded not guilty to all the charges to agree with the statement that the court took insufficient notice of what made them commit the offence.

8.1.2 *Statements which expressed unfavourable attitudes towards the courts*

The majority of defendants in all three groups who chose the venue for their trial expressed agreement with each of the five statements which commented unfavourably on the court systems.

The outstanding feature is the considerable proportions of defendants in all three groups who were critical of magistrates' impartiality. Even among those who chose to be tried by magistrates and whose cases were disposed of by the lower court, 51 per cent agreed strongly that 'magistrates paid more attention to what the police said than to what they said'. The corresponding proportion for those who chose trial on indictment at the Crown Court was 73 per cent, and among those who elected summary trial before magistrates but who were sent to the higher court for sentencing, 73 per cent expressed strong agreement with this statement.

Many defendants also indicated that they were not always able to hear what was being said during their trial, and that they were so overwhelmed that they did not always understand the proceedings. If this is so then it is clearly an unsatisfactory situation and probably puts a defendant at a considerable disadvantage. A simple explanation of court procedure and of what a defendant is expected to do and say in court, before making an appearance, would probably not only help and reassure a large number of defendants, but also, and more important in the light of our findings, might give them more confidence in the legal system.

8.2 Summary

The majority of defendants who chose the venue for their own trial agreed with each statement that expressed an unfavourable attitude towards the court system, which seems to indicate a considerable lack of confidence in the existing procedures at both levels of court. The lack of confidence in the impartiality of magistrates has been discussed earlier in this report when it was reported as being a reason for choosing Crown Court trial, but the fact that over two-thirds of each of the two groups of defendants who chose to appear before magistrates believe that there is a bias towards the police must be a cause for concern.

Some problems would seem to have comparatively simple solutions: for example, the inability of some defendants to hear what was being said is probably easily remedied once the difficulty is appreciated. It has also been suggested that preparing a defendant for what is going to happen when he appears in court might reduce the trauma of a court appearance and because a defendant may then have a better appreciation of what is going on confidence in the system might improve.

8.3 Attitudes to sentencing

8.3.1. *Sentencing by Crown Court judges and by magistrates*

Defendants were asked whether they thought that most magistrates would give about the same sentence for a similar offence or whether it would depend a lot on who heard the case. The question was then repeated but in respect of judges at Crown Courts.

The table shows that the majority of defendants in each of the three groups who chose the venue for their trial thought that different magistrates would vary in the sentence they gave different offenders for similar offences. With the notable exception of those defendants who had been committed from a magistrates' court to the Crown Court for sentence, significantly smaller proportions of defendants in the other two groups thought that Crown Court judges would vary in the sentence they gave different offenders for similar offences. Although the proportions in these groups were smaller, they were nevertheless considerable.

It was thought that defendants who chose to go to the Crown Court for trial might be more likely to think that Crown Court judges would be consistent in their sentencing than defendants who elected to stay and be tried by magistrates; there was no evidence to support this idea.

Table 35 *Proportions of defendants who thought that different magistrates, and different judges, would vary in the sentence they gave for a similar offence: those who chose the venue for their trial*

	Venue for trial chosen by defendant					
	Crown Court		Magistrates' court			
	Disposal at					
	Crown Court		Magistrates' court		Crown Court	
	%	Base[1] = 100%	%	Base[1] = 100%	%	Base[1] = 100%
Different magistrates would vary in the sentence they gave for a similar offence	89	(161)	88	(201)	95	(43)
Different judges would vary in the sentence they gave for a similar offence	77	(159)	71	(200)	98	(43)

() Denotes number not percentage.
[1] Excludes those not answering.

8.3.2 *Defendants' attitudes to their sentences*

Defendants who had been convicted and sentenced either by magistrates or by Crown Court judges were asked about the sentences they were given. In particular they were asked whether they were heavier or lighter than expected and how they thought they would compare with the sentence that might have been passed had they made a different venue decision. It is difficult to draw conclusions from the answers they gave not only because they may have been merely a reflection of the way they felt about their sentence but also because it is almost impossible to assess objectively whether or not a sentence was unduly harsh or light. Nevertheless comparisons between the three sample groups show some interesting differences.

Of the 203 defendants who chose to be tried by magistrates and whose cases were disposed of by the magistrates' court, 96 per cent were convicted on at least one charge and were subsequently sentenced by the magistrates. Of the 166 defendants who chose trial on indictment at the Crown Court, 67 per cent were convicted on at least one charge, and were subsequently sentenced by Crown Court judges. By definition all 43 defendants in the third sample group were convicted by magistrates and subsequently sentenced by judges at the Crown Court.

Table 36 shows the defendant's own assessment of the severity of their sentence. It can be seen that a significantly greater proportion of defendants convicted and sentenced by magistrates compared with those convicted at the Crown Court and sentenced by Crown Court judges received sentences which were, on the whole, what they had expected and that over half of both groups did as well as or better than they had expected. It is also interesting to note that nearly a third of those defendants who had been sent from the magistrates' court to the Crown Court for sentencing also reported that their sentences were about what they had expected, and that again over half of this group did either better or as well as they had expected.

Considering only those defendants whose sentences were in some way different from what they had expected, it was found that there were no significant differences between any of the three groups in the proportions who felt that the sentence they had been given was either heavier or lighter than they had expected. It is worth noting however that of the 43 defendants who chose to be tried by magistrates, who were convicted by them, and then sent to the Crown Court for sentence, as many as 23 per cent said that the sentence they had been given by the Crown Court judge was lighter than they had expected.

The same three groups of defendants were then asked whether they thought their

Table 36 *Defendants' assessment of the severity of their sentence: those who chose the venue for their trial and who were convicted and sentenced on at least one charge*

Defendants' assessment of the severity of their sentence	Venue for trial chosen by defendant		
	Crown Court	Magistrates' court	
	Disposal at		
	Crown Court	Magistrates' court	Crown Court
	%	%	%
The sentence passed was:			
lighter than expected	33	24	23
heavier than expected	41	36	42
about what was expected	20	36	30
Defendant had no idea what to expect	6	5	5
All defendants who chose the venue for their trial and who were convicted and sentenced on at least one charge: base[1]	110 = 100%	194 = 100%	43 = 100%

sentences would have been any heavier or lighter had they been sentenced at the alternative court—table 37. The problems of interpreting this data have already been mentioned but there are nevertheless several points worth noting. First, it is rather surprising to find that the proportion of defendants who had been sentenced by magistrates and who thought that Crown Court judges would have passed a heavier sentence is not larger. The table also shows that over one-third of this group thought that their sentence would have been no different had they gone to the Crown Court, and similarly that about a quarter of those who were convicted at the Crown Court and sentenced by Crown Court judges thought that their sentence would have been no different had they appeared before a magistrates' court.

Table 37 *Defendants' assessment of the possible severity of sentence from the alternative court compared with the sentence they actually received: those who chose the venue for their trial and who were convicted and sentenced on at least one charge*

Defendants' assessment of the possible severity of sentence from the alternative court	Venue for trial chosen by defendant		
	Crown Court	Magistrates' court	
	Disposal at		
	Crown Court	Magistrates' court	Crown Court
	%	%	%
At the alternative court the sentence would have been:			
heavier	41	39	33
lighter	35	24	51
no different	26	37	16
All defendants who chose the venue for their trial and were convicted and sentenced on at least one charge: base[1]	104 = 100%	178 = 100%	43 = 100%

[1] Excludes those not answering.

The other interesting point concerns the group of defendants convicted by magistrates and sent to the Crown Court for sentence: one-third of this group thought that had they been sentenced by the magistrates their sentences would in fact have been heavier than those passed by the higher court judges. Investigation of the sentences that had been passed by the Crown Court judges showed that of the 43 defendants they dealt with, 21 per cent were given sentences which were within the powers of magistrates; prison sentences or suspended sentences of less than six months, and probation orders.

Of this group of 43 defendants, 67 per cent did not expect to be sent to the Crown Court for sentence if they were found guilty of any of the charges against them, and 70 per cent would, in retrospect, have preferred to have had the whole of the case heard at the Crown Court, rather than being sent there just for sentence.

These 30 defendants who in retrospect would have preferred to have had their case heard by Crown Court judges rather than just being sent to the higher court for sentence were asked why they now felt differently about the venue decision they had originally made. Many defendants now wished they had opted for Crown Court trial because it would have been fairer. Since all these defendants had pleaded guilty to all charges, with the exception of one who pleaded guilty to only some of the charges against him, a fairer trial probably meant a more thorough hearing of their case. Indeed one-third of this group of 30 defendants specifically mentioned that they wished they had gone to the Crown Court because they thought they would have had a better and more thorough hearing with more attention being paid to what they had to say. Six defendants wished they had opted for Crown Court trial because they thought that ultimately it would have been quicker to have gone to the Crown Court in the first place; this was their only reason for preferring trial at a higher court. Three defendants thought that judges would have been better qualified to hear their cases and two defendants would have preferred Crown Court trial because they could have been represented. A further two defendants said that they would have changed their plea to not guilty, had an alibi and called witnesses at the Crown Court. They had originally chosen summary trial before magistrates, because, among other reasons, they wanted their cases to be dealt with quickly. One other defendant answered as follows:

'It must be better to have it all heard at the Crown Court, to keep the case altogether at the Crown Court, otherwise I think some of the truth can be lost travelling from one court to another'.

Defendants whose cases were tried and disposed of at the venue of their choice, were asked whether they thought in certain circumstances, magistrates should be able to send defendants who had chosen to be tried by them to a higher court for sentence. Just under half the defendants in both groups agreed that as under the present system magistrates should continue to be able to commit some defendants to the Crown Court for sentencing by Crown Court judges.[1]

8.4 Improvements to court procedure suggested by defendants

All defendants were asked whether or not they had found the experience of going to court on this occasion an ordeal. Of the 166 defendants who chose to go to the Crown Court for trial, 78 per cent[2] reported that their trial had been an ordeal; of the 203 defendants who chose to be tried at a magistrates' court, and whose cases were disposed of by the magistrates, 66 per cent found the experience an ordeal,[3] and of the 43 defendants who chose to be tried by magistrates, but who were sent to the Crown Court for sentence, 63 per cent found going to court on that particular occasion an ordeal.[4] These three groups of defendants were subsequently asked what they thought could be done to make the experience less of an ordeal. Table 38 shows the improvements that were suggested.

The two most striking features of the table are the considerable proportions of defendants in all three groups who were unhappy about the time it had taken to deal with

---

[1] See table C14, p 82.
[2] Base for percentage excludes five defendants who did not answer.
[3] Base for percentage excludes three defendants who did not answer.
[4] Defendants who reported being given no choice of venue for their trial were also asked whether going to court had, on this occasion, been an ordeal. It was interesting to find that these defendants were no more likely to have found appearing at court an ordeal than those who chose the venue for their trial themselves; see table C13, p 82.

their case, either at a magistrates' court or at the Crown Court, and the similarly high proportions of defendants who, although they felt the whole experience was an ordeal, could think of no way to improve the situation. It was noted earlier that there were indications that some defendants had been unable to hear all that was being said in court, and that others could not understand the proceedings as they found the whole thing overwhelming. It was not surprising therefore to find that among the suggested improvements to court procedure were better explanations of court procedure and of a defendant's rights. Having a less formal atmosphere in court, including doing away with wigs and gowns, and reducing the amount of technical jargon used, all suggested by defendants, would also probably make the experience less overwhelming and perhaps lead to a better understanding of what goes on in court.

Table 38 *Improvements to court procedure suggested by defendants who chose the venue for their trial and who found the experience of going to court an ordeal*

The experience of going to court was an ordeal and could have been made less so by . . .	Venue for trial chosen by defendant		
	Crown Court	Magistrates' court	
	Disposal at		
	Crown Court	Magistrates' court	Crown Court
	%	%	%
Dealing with the case more quickly	51	31	33
Having a less formal atmosphere in court	17	15	7
Better facilities at court: waiting room, refreshment facilities, etc.	11	9	4
Better explanation of what was going to happen in court	9	9	4
More privacy in court, no reporters, no spectators	5	15	7
Better explanation of one's 'rights'	5	7	4
Other answers	14	3	37
Nothing could be done, don't know, no idea what should happen	30	53	41
All defendants who chose the venue for their trial and who found the experience of going to court an ordeal: base	126 = 100%	132 = 100%	27 = 100%

All 10 of the answers included in the category of 'other answers' for defendants who had been tried by magistrates but sent to the Crown Court for sentence concerned the greater availability of remand on bail rather than in custody. The 'other answers' for the remaining two groups included having more time and freedom to discuss the case with counsel during the proceedings, as in the USA, having more notice of when the trial is to take place, and not being locked up during the court adjournments.

9 Summary

The main purpose of this survey was to find out why, when given an option of venue for their trial, some defendants chose trial at a magistrates' court, while others were prepared to wait a considerable length of time, perhaps in custody, for their case to be heard at the Crown Court before a judge and jury.

9.1 The sample and survey method

The information was obtained by interviewing defendants in cases which had recently been disposed of at either a magistrates' court or at one of the Crown Court centres in the Greater London area. Three samples were selected from records held at the courts: one sample was of defendants whose cases had been tried and disposed of at the Crown Court, the second was a sample of defendants whose cases had been tried and disposed of at magistrates' courts, and the third sample was of defendants who had been tried and convicted by magistrates, but who had been sent to the Crown Court for sentence. Interviews were achieved with 262 defendants whose cases had been tried and disposed of at the Crown Court, with 225 defendants whose cases had been tried and disposed of at magistrates' courts and with 57 defendants who had been tried summarily by magistrates and committed to the Crown Court for sentence. These numbers represent 71 per cent, 66 per cent and 73 per cent of the total numbers of interviews attempted in each of the three sample groups respectively. Although the response rates were lower than would normally be expected, no marked differences were found between the respondent groups and the groups of non-responders which might invalidate any conclusions based on the results of this enquiry.

At present not all offences carry a venue option, and for some that do it is not always a venue option for the defendant: for some offences it is the prosecution or the bench who are able to determine at which level of court the case will be heard. The three samples selected were of 'defendant-cases' where at least one offence in the case carried a venue option. This meant that some defendants who were interviewed had not exercised the venue option themselves but were tried summarily at a magistrates' court or on indictment at the Crown Court as a result of a request by the prosecution. Of the total numbers of defendants successfully interviewed in each of the sample groups, 37 per cent of defendants whose cases were tried and disposed of at the Crown Court, 10 per cent of defendants whose cases were tried and disposed of at magistrates' courts and 25 per cent of defendants who were tried by magistrates but sentenced by Crown Court judges reported having had no personal choice of venue for their trial. It was estimated that each of these groups probably included between 8 per cent and 25 per cent of defendants who, although they were actually responsible for determining the venue for their trial themselves, had failed to appreciate the part they had played.

The remaining 166 defendants whose cases were tried and disposed of at the Crown Court, 203 defendants whose cases were tried and disposed of at magistrates' courts, and 43 defendants tried by magistrates and sentenced by judges, reported that the venue for their trial had been their own choice.

9.2 The plea

It was found that the distribution of guilty pleas and not guilty pleas between those who chose to be tried at a magistrates' court and those who chose to be tried at the Crown Court was overwhelmingly different. Of the 203 defendants who chose to be tried at a magistrates' court and whose cases were disposed of by the magistrates, only 6 per cent pleaded not guilty to all charges; none of the 43 defendants who were committed to the Crown Court for sentence after choosing to be tried at a magistrates' court pleaded not guilty to all charges at the lower court. In marked contrast, of the

166 defendants who chose to be tried at the Crown Court, 69 per cent pleaded not guilty to all the charges against them. However, the enquiry found that, at the time the decision to go to the Crown Court was made, an even higher proportion, 85 per cent, had intended to plead not guilty: between making a venue decision and appearing at the Crown Court 26 defendants decided to change their plea to one of guilty. Thus taking into account what defendants intended to do at the time they made their venue decision there is an even more marked difference in the distribution of pleas.

9.3 Reasons for choosing to be tried by magistrates or at the Crown Court

The reasons that defendants gave for making a particular venue decision were found to have a strong association with plea. Defendants who chose to go to the Crown Court for trial were in the main contesting the charges against them, and had chosen the higher court because they wanted a more thorough hearing than they believed they would have been given at a magistrates' court. They wanted a judge and jury to listen to their case, and to have the best chance of acquittal. It appeared that some defendants had been unwilling to take a contested case before magistrates because they felt them to be biased in favour of the police, and because they lacked confidence in 'untrained' justices. This contrasts with the reasons for choosing summary trial at a magistrates' court. The majority of these defendants were pleading guilty and wanted to be dealt with in the shortest possible time and have the best chance of a light sentence.

The majority of defendants seemed to be aware of the implications of their choice and had sufficient knowledge of the two court systems to be able to make a reasoned choice between them. Only 13 per cent of defendants who chose trial on indictment at the Crown Court, and 23 per cent of those who chose summary trial at a magistrates' court and whose cases were disposed of by magistrates, had never been to court before for any reason. This previous experience, and the previous experience that over 60 per cent of defendants in each of the three groups who chose the venue for their trial had as previous offenders had probably contributed to their knowledge of the two court systems and their attitudes towards the two levels of court. There was no evidence to suggest that by improving defendant's knowledge of the differences in procedure and of the different powers of the two courts to deal with offenders, substantial numbers who would have previously chosen trial on indictment at the Crown Court, would then opt for summary trial before magistrates. Of the 166 defendants who chose trial at the Crown Court a maximum of 17 would have made a different venue decision had their knowledge of magistrates' courts been better, and of the 203 defendants who had been dealt with summarily by magistrates a maximum of 27 would have opted for Crown Court trial with improved knowledge.

9.4 Importance of the venue option

Being given a choice of venue on this occasion was generally important to defendants in all three groups. Among the defendants who felt that the choice of venue had been unimportant very few said that they felt this way because they thought the outcome would have been the same whichever court they went to.

Apart from the venue option for their own case being regarded by some defendants as important, there was also concern that persons charged with other offences should be allowed to choose the venue for their trial. From a range of nine offences—varying in degrees of seriousness, some of which do not currently carry an option, there were indications that the more serious an offence was regarded by a defendant, the more likely was there to be a feeling that a venue option for the accused was important. But even for the offence of 'not having a television licence', which was regarded as serious by less than 10 per cent of any group, at least one-third of defendants in each of the three groups who chose the venue for their own trial thought that an option of venue for trial on the part of a person accused of such an offence was important.

9.5 Defendants' attitudes to their trial

By asking for defendants' reactions to a number of statements relating to court procedure and to appearing for trial at either a magistrates' court or the Crown Court, some indications of defendants' feelings about their trial were obtained. Several aspects of their trial had obviously caused concern to appreciable numbers of defendants; about one-third of defendants in each of the three groups who chose the venue for their trial agreed with a statement which indicated that they had been unable to hear all that was being said in court; similar proportions were apparently so overwhelmed by the proceedings that they could not always understand what was happening.

The level of confidence in the courts and in their ability to deal fairly with defendants did not seem particularly high: over two-thirds of defendants in each of the three sample groups who chose the venue for their trial agreed with the statement put to them that magistrates' courts were police courts, and the suggestion that a defendant always gets a fair trial was rejected by over half the defendants in each group. Over one-third of defendants in each group also disagreed with the statement 'one is innocent until proved guilty'. It should be noted that a somewhat small proportion of defendants who chose to go to the Crown Court for trial (35 per cent) spontaneously mentioned that one reason why they had made such a choice was because they believed magistrates' courts to be 'police courts'.

9.6 Defendants' suggestions for improving court procedure

Well over half the defendants in each of the three groups who had chosen the venue for their trial had, on this occasion, found the experience of going to court an ordeal. The most frequent spontaneous suggestion for what could have made it less of an ordeal was to reduce the amount of time it had taken to deal with their case. Defendants who chose to be tried by magistrates and whose cases were disposed of by them, were generally dealt with much more quickly than defendants in either of the other two groups who chose the venue for their trial, and it was interesting to find therefore that all three groups mentioned being dealt with more speedily as something that would have made the experience less of an ordeal.

Making the proceedings less formal, for example by doing away with wigs and gowns and by reducing the use of technical jargon, and more explanation of court procedure would also have made the experience of appearing at court less of an ordeal for many defendants.

However defendants generally seemed to be satisfied with the choice of venue they had made for their trial and with the hearing they had received. Over three-quarters of both those defendants who chose to be tried at the Crown Court and those who chose to be tried at a magistrates' court and whose cases were disposed of by the lower court said that looking back on their case now that it was over they would still have made the same choice of venue.

Appendix A

Current Classification of Offences

INDICTABLE OFFENCES

SUMMARY OFFENCES

HYBRID OFFENCES

1 INDICTABLE OFFENCES

1.1 Indictable offences which can be tried only on indictment

The most serious indictable offences which can be tried only on indictment, such as murder, rape and blackmail, can only be tried by a judge at a Crown Court. A defendant charged with such an offence will first appear at a magistrates' court before magistrates, acting as examining justices, who will commit him for trial to the Crown Court. At the Crown Court his case is heard by a judge and a jury, a verdict is reached and if it is one of guilty, sentence is passed by the Crown Court judge.

1.2 Indictable offences which can be tried summarily

For some offences the defendant may be given the option of being tried summarily at a magistrates' court, where the maximum penalty is limited to six months' imprisonment, a fine of £400, or both. Examples of indictable offences that can be tried summarily with the consent of the accused are theft, inflicting grievous bodily harm and criminal damage. A full list of these offences is set out in the first schedule to the Magistrates' Courts Act 1952, as amended. For these offences the procedure governing the mode of trial is·covered by s.19 of the Act. This allows for the magistrates to begin as examining justices, that is as if they were going to commit the defendant for trial to the Crown Court, but they may at any time, with the consent of the accused, change to summary trial. Before the magistrates can begin summary trial they must however be satisfied that, 'having regard to any representations made in the presence of the accused by the prosecutor, or made by the accused, and to the nature of the case, that the punishment the court has power to inflict (on summary trial) . . . would be adequate and that the circumstances do not make the offence one of serious character and do not for other reasons require trial on indictment'.[1]

Generally the procedure is as follows; the prosecution initially requests summary trial, possibly giving reasons for doing so, the magistrates offer no objection, and then the consent of the accused is sought. The agreement of the magistrates and the consent of the defendant are both essential. If no request is made for summary trial by the prosecution, or if the magistrates refuse to allow summary trial, or if the defendant withholds his consent, then the magistrates revert to acting as examining magistrates with a view to committing the defendant for trial at the Crown Court.

Additionally, if the defendant does consent to summary trial by the magistrates and is subsequently convicted by them, he may, if the magistrates deem it necessary, be committed to the Crown Court for sentence under s.29 of the Act. Defendants are informed of the possibility of being committed to the Crown Court for sentence when they are asked whether or not they consent to summary trial.

2 SUMMARY OFFENCES

2.1 Summary offences which can only be tried summarily

These generally carry a maximum penalty of three months or less on conviction, and include parking offences, speeding, and being drunk and disorderly. A defendant charged with such an offence must have his case tried and disposed of at the magistrates' court.

2.2. Summary offences which can be tried on indictment

For some summary offences, generally those which carry a maximum penalty of more than three months' imprisonment, the defendant is entitled to choose to go to the Crown Court for trial before a judge and jury. Examples are, illegal entry (Immigration Act 1971 s.24), and possessing a firearm without a certificate. For such offences the

---

[1] Magistrates' Courts Act 1952 s.19(2).

venue for trial is determined entirely by the defendant: his wishes cannot be overruled by either the prosecution or the magistrates, and a choice of summary trial would not generally make a convicted defendant liable for committal for sentence to the Crown Court. The procedure governing the mode of trial is covered by s.25 of the 1952 Act.

3 HYBRID OFFENCES

These are offences that are not included in either of the two categories above, and they are, by statutory provision, triable either summarily or on indictment, and as such they carry different maximum penalties according to where the trial of the offence takes place. The procedure governing the mode of trial of such offences is set out in s.18 of the 1952 Act.

For hybrid offences the magistrates proceed as examining justices, *unless*, before any evidence is heard, the prosecution requests summary trial and the magistrates agree. With a few exceptions if the defendant is charged with a hybrid offence that carries a maximum of more than three months' imprisonment on summary conviction, and the prosecution has made an application for summary trial which has been accepted by the magistrates, then the defendant may either consent to summary trial or ask to be committed for trial to the Crown Court, in which event the magistrates revert to acting as examining justices with a view to committal for trial. If however the defendant agrees to summary trial, he is not liable to be committed to the Crown Court for sentence under s.29 of the 1952 Act. There is however a further provision which allows for a summary trial, proceeding in this way, to be discontinued at any point before the conclusion of evidence for the prosecution, and for the magistrates to revert to acting as examining justices.

If, however, the magistrates have begun to act as examining justices, they may, at any time, change to summary trial, having regard to representations made by the prosecution, or the defendant, and the nature of the case. But before summary trial can proceed in this way, if, with certain exceptions, the offence is punishable on summary conviction by a sentence of more than three months, then again the defendant's consent must be obtained. If the defendant's agreement is obtained and summary trial proceeds in this way, then a defendant subsequently convicted is liable for committal to the Crown Court for sentence under s.29 of the 1952 Act. If, however, the defendant asks for trial at the Crown Court then the magistrates revert to acting as examining justices with a view to committal for trial.

For hybrid offences that carry a maximum of three months' imprisonment or less on summary conviction the defendant has no right to claim trial at a Crown Court: examples are, possessing an offensive weapon, and threatening etc. behaviour likely to cause a breach of the peace. Dangerous driving, possessing a controlled drug, and 'drinking and driving' are examples of hybrid offences carrying a maximum of more than three months' imprisonment on summary conviction.

Appendix B

Further details of the sample selection and the response

SAMPLE REQUIREMENTS

The survey required a sample of individuals aged 17 and over who had been defendants in criminal cases. It was limited to those defendants who were charged with at least one offence of the type which carries an 'option of venue' that is, a summary offence which could be tried on indictment at the Crown Court, an indictable offence which could be tried summarily at a magistrates' court, or a hybrid offence which could be heard either at the Crown Court or at a magistrates' court. Only those defendants whose cases were completed, that is, verdict brought and sentence or order given were to be included. The sample was to be confined further to those defendants whose cases were completed in courts in the Greater London area.

Size

It was estimated that about 800 interviews could be attempted, and because the intention was to compare the views of defendants who had been tried at magistrates' courts with those of defendants who had been tried at the Crown Court, approximately equal numbers of these two groups of defendants were needed for interview. However, it became apparent at a quite early stage of the survey that a third sample of defendants would be required: this would comprise defendants who had been tried and convicted by magistrates, but who were then committed for sentence to the Crown Court. The overall estimated sample size was not increased to allow for this third sample, but remained at about 800.

THE SAMPLE FRAME

There were, ostensibly, several sets of records which could have been used as a sampling frame for defendants:

Police records;
Central records held by Home Office Statistical Branch;
Court records.

Police records have disadvantages. The number of police stations holding records of cases heard in Greater London is relatively large and thus the records themselves are widely dispersed. With the time constraints imposed on the survey it would have been necessary to take a small proportion of police stations as primary sampling units, and there would have been difficulties in compiling sufficient statistical data to stratify the police stations before the sample selection could be made. It was also felt that acceptance by an informant of the independant nature of the enquiry could be jeopardised if it were known that names had been obtained from police records. Not all defendants are brought to court by the police and those prosecuted by other individuals or groups are not therefore recorded by the police: the number of such cases is however thought to be minimal.

Nevertheless because of these conditions and restraints the possibility of access to police records was not pursued.

Home Office records are compiled from returns sent in regularly by the police and are therefore subject to some of the same deficiencies. However their over-riding disadvantage is the omission of defendants' addresses and, on some returns, the lack of names.

Our research suggested that court records would be the most suitable of the three sources from which to draw the samples.

Criminal courts are less numerous than police stations in the Greater London area, their records of recently completed cases are comprehensive and all relevant details about defendants required for sampling purposes are available from them. It was decided therefore, with the agreement of the Lord Chancellors' Office and the clerks of Court at magistrates' courts, to use court records as a sampling frame.

Deficiencies of the frame

Court records were not without their disadvantages as a sampling frame, the problems being different in the Crown Court and in magistrates' courts.

Crown Court Records

At each Crown Court centre a separate file is kept for each separate case, but because one case may involve more than one defendant a sample of case files would be expected to yield a larger sample of defendants. However, case files contain all the information necessary for sampling purposes, including the name(s) and address(es) of the defendant(s), the charge(s) and the verdict(s) and sentence(s) or order(s) given. The case files are kept in order of date of committal to the Crown Court for trial, *not* the date of completion of cases. The period between committal for trial and first appearance at the Crown Court varies considerably, as does the length of hearing: some cases are adjourned or sentence is deferred for relatively long periods. As the survey was concerned with defendants whose cases had been disposed of, there was either the problem of deciding how far back to go in the records in order to ensure the inclusion of all cases which were concluded by a certain date, or if the sample were restricted to cases committed over a short period of time, there was the problem of determining the sampling fraction.

Magistrates' Court Records

A daily record of cases brought before a magistrates' court is kept in the Court Register. It is laid down by statute that certain details of each case, such as the defendants' name, the charge and the adjudication, should be recorded in the register. From a sampling point of view, the vital details which the registers are not required to contain, and which many do not contain, is the address of the defendant. Because of this it was decided that in magistrates' courts an alternative frame, the 'charge' and 'summons' sheets, would have to be used. Charge sheets, containing personal details of defendants as well as details of the charges, are made out by the police after arrest. Summonses are prepared usually as a result of apprehensions by the police in duplicate and one copy is sent by the courts themselves to defendants; the other copy is retained by the court. Summonses contain fewer, but still adequate, personal details. Charge sheets however are police property and are returned to them, often immediately after the case is completed.

THE SAMPLE DESIGN

The sample was to be in two stages with courts as primary sampling units, and defendants in relevant cases completed in these courts as the final stage.

To overcome some of the problems inherent in using court records it was decided to determine a relatively short time period during which defendants in cases completed would form the basis of the sample to be interviewed.

Selection of primary units

Crown Court Centres

There are eight Crown Courts in Greater London, one of which deals solely with civil cases. As this was outside the terms of reference of the survey it was excluded and, the seven remaining Crown Court centres were treated as the primary sampling units.

Magistrates' Courts

The 41 magistrates' courts in Greater London were arranged by court division, thus introducing some geographical stratification, and then alternate courts were selected yielding a sample of 20 magistrates' courts. The clerk at one of the selected courts was unwilling to co-operate in the enquiry and the sample was therefore reduced to 19.

Selection of defendants from primary units

From information obtained from the Home Office and from the courts themselves it was estimated that in order to achieve the required samples of about 400 defendants from the Crown Court and magistrates' courts respectively, sampling should take place over a period of two weeks in each of the Crown Court centres and for three days in each of the magistrates' courts. To complete the survey in the required time, the two week period 11 March–23 March 1974 was selected for sampling. It was decided that the sample should consist of defendants in all relevant cases completed throughout the whole of this period in each of the Crown Court centres and on three days, during the same two week period in each of the magistrates' courts selected.

Since the samples were to include only those defendants whose cases had been completed, defendants tried and convicted at magistrates' courts and sentenced at the Crown Court were selected from records held at the Crown Court centres. The method of selecting the samples had the incidental advantage of producing a rather larger number of this third group of defendants than would have been obtained by sampling magistrates' courts' records and constituted an adequate third sample.

NOTE:

The samples from each level of court were designed to be self-weighting but as the sampling fractions used to select defendants from magistrates' courts and from the Crown Court centres in the Greater London area were different the samples are not directly additive.

RETURNS FROM THE COURTS

All the Crown Court centres and all but one of the magistrates' courts agreed to co-operate in the survey. Four magistrates' courts had annexes which were administered separately, but two of these dealt entirely with cases with which the survey was not concerned (domestic proceedings and juvenile cases). Thus seven Crown Court centres and 21 magistrates' courts and annexes remained as first-stage units. Two magistrates' courts drew samples on days they had not been allocated but, as the overall samples were small, and it would have been virtually impossible to re-sample for the correct days, those sampled on the wrong days were accepted. There was nothing to suggest that this introduced any bias into the samples. One magistrates' court was sampled on two days only, as other days were irrelevant.

Saturdays were included in the magistrates' court sample only half as often as weekdays, as only half of the London magistrates' courts held petty sessions on Saturdays.

Details were returned from the courts for a total of 948 defendant cases; 141 were withdrawn from this original return leaving 807 defendants available for interview.

Table B1 gives the original sample sizes for each of the samples, and the reasons for exclusion of the 141 defendant-cases.

Details of 489 'defendant-cases' were returned from the Crown Court centres for cases which had been tried and disposed of in the higher courts. As this made the interview sample too large 72 defendant-cases were eliminated at random to reduce the size. A further 69 defendant-cases were withdrawn from the samples and in most cases the reasons for these withdrawals are self explanatory from the table. Those defendants who had no address, and one defendant with an address in the USA, obviously could not be traced or interviewed and were therefore withdrawn prior to fieldwork. Defendants committed to a mental hospital, and one defendant whom the court felt was of an unstable character were also excluded.

Eight defendants could not be traced either because of a mistake made in the address

Table B1 *Original sample sizes and reasons for exclusion of 141 defendant-cases from the original returns made by the courts*

	Venue for trial		
	Crown Court	Magistrates' court	
	Disposal at		
	Crown Court	Magistrates' court	Crown Court
	Nos	Nos	Nos
Original number of 'defendant-cases' returned from courts	489	366	93
Eliminated at random to reduce size	72	—	—
Number of 'defendant-cases' remaining	417	366	93
Of no fixed abode	7	13	7
No address—court records inadequate/omitted in error	4	4	—
Address outside United Kingdom	—	1	—
Not to be interviewed—subject to hospital order	4	—	2
Duplicates: defendants appearing on more than one occasion	22	1	4
Number of defendants selected for interview	380	347	80

when sampling, or because a prison address was all that was recorded and defendants were subsequently found to have been discharged but no private address was available.

Some defendants had appeared in court in different cases on more than one occasion during the sampling period. Twenty-six defendants had appeared twice in the two week period, and one on three occasions each for different cases. Because the final sample unit was of defendant-cases, these 27 defendants should have been included in the sample and interviewed about each case separately. This was impracticable and so interviewers were given details of all a defendant's cases, but were told to carry out an interview in relation to only one case, which had been chosen at random.

THE RESPONSE

Interviewers were required to contact all defendants in each sample either at their home address or at a penal institution. If an interviewer discovered that a sampled defendant had been arrested on a new charge and was awaiting trial in connection with the offence, then the interviewer was instructed not to proceed with the interview and that defendant was withdrawn from the sample. Five defendants were not interviewed for this reason.

A further nine defendants were found to be ineligible for interview and were also withdrawn from the samples at this stage. Four had the charges against them withdrawn and no plea had been taken from them when they appeared at court, three defendants were aged under 17, one defendant was subject to a deferred sentence and his case was therefore regarded as unfinished on the date of sampling, and one remaining defendant had his case completed on a date outside the specified sampling period and had been included in error.

One defendant had been deported and was withdrawn from the sample.

Therefore, including the five defendants who were awaiting trial on new charges, in all, 15 defendants were withdrawn from the samples leaving a total of 792 defendants to be interviewed.

Full interviews were obtained with 544 defendants; this represents 69 per cent of the total number issued for interview.

The reasons for non-interview fall broadly into two categories; refusals and non-contacts. Table B2 gives a full analysis of response and reasons for non-interview for the three samples.

Table B2 *Analysis of response and reasons for non-interview for the three samples of defendants*

	Venue for trial				
	Crown Court	Magistrates' court			
	Disposal at				
	Crown Court	Magistrates' court		Crown Court	
Total sample of defendants	380	347		80	
Defendants subsequently ineligible for interview					
(i) no case to answer	2	2		—	
(ii) too young	1	—		2	
(iii) case incomplete	—	1		—	
(iv) outside sampling period	1	—		—	
(v) being held on new charge	4	1		—	
(vi) deported	1	—		—	
	Nos	%	Nos	%	Nos	%
Effective sample set	371	100	343	100	78	100
Interviews achieved	262	71	225	66	57	73
Reasons for non-interview						
(i) interview refused	18	5	32	9	3	4
(ii) gone home, outside United Kingdom	7		6		—	
(iii) left prison, now no fixed address	—		2		1	
(iv) left prison, absconded	1		—		—	
(v) address empty/demolished	8	5	7	5	1	4
(vi) non-existent address	2		—		—	
(vii) non-private address	1		2		1	
(viii) language difficulties	1		2		—	
(ix) known at address, but no forwarding address available	34		26		6	
(x) not known at address	5		9		3	
(xi) out each call, known to be resident	21	19	17	19	4	19
(xii) out each call, don't know whether resident	5		6		1	
(xiii) convenience address	5		7		1	
(xiv) other non-contacts	1	*	2	1	—	—

The non-interview rate of 31 per cent, representing 254 defendants, was higher than normally expected. However it was felt that the subject matter of the enquiry might have led to more refusals than normally anticipated, and also that a sample of defendants might be more difficult to trace than a sample of the general population. Bearing these two points in mind, the number of interviews achieved did not fall short of expectations. The proportions of non-responders in the three samples are nevertheless considerable and are worth looking at in some detail.

---

* Less than 1 per cent.

Those who refused to co-operate in the enquiry

Overall the refusal rate was less than had been feared; 53 people refused to co-operate in the enquiry, 32 of whom were defendants in cases heard at magistrates' courts.

Three types of refusal were encountered: refusals direct to the interviewer by the sampled defendant, which accounted for the majority of refusals, refusals by some other member of the household, on behalf of the sampled defendant, and those classified as 'tacit' refusals by reason of broken appointment. The two main reasons for not wanting to co-operate in the study were that it would be too distressing to talk about the case, it was best forgotten—this reason being especially frequent from female defendants, and secondly, a general dislike of the treatment that had been received from the courts and a dislike of British justice in general. Very few defendants were not interested in the survey to the extent of refusing an interview, and fewer still refused as a matter of principle in that they were anti- all surveys or anti- the Government.

Table B3 shows the numbers of men and women in each of the three samples who refused to co-operate in the enquiry, and for comparison, the proportions of men and women in various other sub-groups in each of the three samples.

Table B3 *Distribution of men and women in various sub-groups according to venue for trial*

	Venue for trial					
	Crown Court		Magistrates' court			
	Disposal at					
	Crown Court		Magistrates' court		Crown Court	
	Men	Women	Men	Women	Men	Women
Refusals	(15)	(3)	(19)	(13)	(3)	—
	%	%	%	%	%	%
Interviews attempted	90	10	80	20	89	11
Interviews achieved	90	10	82	18	86	14
Non-contacts, excluding refusals	88	12	83	17	94	6

() Denotes number not percentage.

Although the base numbers are small, it can be seen that the proportion of women whose cases had been tried and disposed of at magistrates' courts and who refused to co-operate in the enquiry was significantly greater than the proportion of women in other sub-groups in that sample. Nearly one in five of the women whose cases had been tried and disposed of at magistrates' courts and who were selected for interview refused to co-operate, and although the actual numbers involved are small since the proportion is high it is worth briefly examining this special sub-group of 13 women.

Of the 13 women whose cases had been tried and disposed of by magistrates and who refused an interview, nine were charged with shoplifting, two with dishonestly obtaining pecuniary advantage, one with criminal damage, and one with dishonestly handling stolen goods. Ten pleaded guilty and were found guilty; eight women were fined, one was given a probation order, and one a conditional discharge for two years. Five of the nine women charged with shoplifting were over the age of 50, two were under 20 years of age, and the average age of the sub-group was over 40. Ten of the women said that talking about the experience would be too upsetting for them, and in four of these cases the interviewers withdrew to avoid causing further distress. ·

The non-contacts

Table B2 clearly shows that for all three samples the two main reasons for non-contact were a refusal to co-operate in the study (discussed above) and a defendant moving and leaving no forwarding address. Instances where a sampled defendant was known to be resident at the given address, but was not contacted also account for a large proportion of non-contacts. Where the reason for non-response is given as 'convenience address' the sampled defendant had never been resident at the address given—usually a relative's address—but had quoted it when charged with an offence in preference to being recorded as 'of no fixed above'.

Thirteen sampled defendants were not contacted because they had left this country to return home. Of the seven defendants in this group who had been tried at the Crown Court, five had previous convictions for which they had served custodial sentences, and five had pleaded guilty to all charges. All six defendants in this group of non-contacts whose cases had been tried and disposed of by magistrates, pleaded guilty to all the charges against them. Overall there were 11 charges of theft; burglary, possessing a controlled drug, and dishonestly gaining pecuniary advantage each accounted for two charges, and there was one charge of assault occasioning actual bodily harm, of handling stolen goods, of 'taking and driving' and of driving with excess alcohol in the body.

Since the proportion of non-respondents in each of the three samples was higher than is normally accepted as being unlikely to affect the results of an enquiry or any conclusions drawn, non-respondents and respondents were compared on a number of variables for which data was available for the non-respondent groups from the court records. Comparisons for all three sample groups showed that there were no marked differences between non-respondents on the basis of sex, plea or verdict. Defendants whose cases were tried and disposed of at the Crown Court were also compared on the basis of previous convictions and previous custodial sentences, and here again no marked differences were found between the respondent and non-respondent groups. The comparable data for non-respondent defendants tried at magistrates courts was not available. There is, however, no reason to suppose either that defendants who were interviewed are not representative of the three samples selected for interview, or that the considerable proportions of non-respondents will invalidate any conclusions drawn.

Appendix C

Additional tables

Table C1 *Venue for trial that defendants would have chosen had they been given the option: those who reported being given no choice of venue for their trial*

	Venue for trial		
	Crown Court	Magistrates' court	
	Disposal at		
	Crown Court	Magistrates' court	Crown Court
	%	%	
Crown Court	37	33	(7)
Magistrates' court	63	67	(6)
All defendants who reported having no choice of venue for their trial: base[1]	95 = 100%	21 = 100%	(13)

Table C2 *Proportions of defendants found guilty of some or all of the charges against them: those who chose to be tried at the Crown Court and who pleaded guilty to some or all of the charges against them[2]*

Verdict	Defendant pleaded			All defendants who chose Crown Court trial
	Guilty to all charges	Not guilty to all charges	Guilty to only some charges	
	%	%	%	%
Guilty of all charges	100	33	20	46
Not guilty of all charges	—	48	—	33
Guilty of only some charges	—	19	80	21
Number on which percentage based	36=100%	115=100%	15=100%	166=100%

Table C3 *Proportions of defendants found guilty of some or all of the charges against them: those who chose to be tried at a magistrates' court, whose cases were disposed of by the magistrates, and who pleaded guilty to some or all of the charges against them*

Verdict	Defendant pleaded			All defendants who chose trial at a magistrates' court
	Guilty to all charges	Not guilty to all charges	Guilty to only some charges	
	%			%
Guilty of all charges	100	(9)	(3)	95
Not guilty of all charges	—	(4)	—	2
Guilty of only some charges	—	—	(6)	3
Number on which percentage based[1]	179 = 100%	13 = 100%	9 = 100%	201 = 100%

() Denotes number not percentage.
[1] Excludes those not answering.
[2] In this analysis the actual plea entered against the charges has been used.

Table C4 *Proportions of defendants who pleaded guilty to some or all of the charges against them who would still choose to be tried at the Crown Court: those whose cases were tried and disposed of at the Crown Court*

Venue for trial that defendant would now choose	Pleaded		All defendants who chose Crown Court trial
	Not guilty to all charges	Guilty to some or all charges	
	%	%	%
Crown Court	88	76	85
Magistrates' court	10	24	14
Not bothered	2	—	1
Number on which percentage based[1]	113 = 100%	49 = 100%	162 = 100%

Table C5 *Proportions of defendants found guilty of some or all of the charges against them, who would still choose to be tried at the Crown Court: those whose cases were tried and disposed of at the Crown Court*

Venue for trial that defendant would now choose	Verdict		All defendants who chose Crown Court trial
	Not guilty of all charges	Guilty of some or all charges	
	%	%	%
Crown Court	98	78	85
Magistrates' court	—	21	14
Not bothered	2	1	1
Number on which percentage based[1]	55 = 100%	107 = 100%	162 = 100%

Table C6 *Proportions of defendants who pleaded not guilty to some or all of the charges against them who would still choose to be tried at a magistrates' court: those whose cases were tried and disposed of by magistrates*

Venue for trial that defendant would now choose	Pleaded		All defendants who chose trial at a magistrates' court
	Guilty to all charges	Not guilty to some or all charges	
	%	%	%
Crown Court	14	17	14
Magistrates' court	83	79	82
Not bothered	3	4	3
Number on which percentage based[1]	179 = 100%	24 = 100%	203 = 100%

---

[1] Excludes those not answering.

Table C7 *Proportions of defendants found not guilty of some or all of the charges against them who would still choose to be tried at a magistrates' court: those cases were tried and disposed of by magistrates*

Venue for trial that defendant would now choose	Verdict		All defendants who chose trial at a magistrates' court
	Guilty of all charges	Not guilty of some or all charges	
	%		%
Crown Court	13	(3)	14
Magistrates' court	84	(6)	83
Not bothered	3	(1)	3
Number on which percentage based[1]	191 = 100%	10 = 100%	201 = 100%

Table C8 *Period between committal to the Crown Court and the final disposal of the case for defendants who pleaded not guilty to all the charges against them: those who chose to be tried at the Crown Court and whose cases were tried and disposed of at the higher court (cumulative percentages)*

Period between committal and final disposal	Pleaded		All defendants who chose Crown Court trial
	Not guilty to all charges	Guilty to some or all charges	
	cum %	cum %	cum %
Less than 4 weeks	—	—	—
4 weeks to less than 8 weeks	6	10	7
8 weeks to less than 12 weeks	10	14	12
12 weeks to less than 16 weeks	15	36	21
16 weeks to less than 20 weeks	29	56	37
20 weeks to less than 24 weeks	40	64	47
24 weeks to less than 28 weeks	49	68	55
28 weeks to less than 32 weeks	69	76	71
32 weeks to less than 36 weeks	79	90	82
36 weeks to less than 44 weeks	86	96	89
44 weeks or longer	100	100	100
Number on which percentage based[1]	115 = 100%	50 = 100%	165 = 100%

() Denotes number not percentage.
[1] Excludes those not answering.

Table C9 *Period between first appearance and final disposal of case for defendants who pleaded not guilty to some or all the charges against them: those who chose to be tried at a magistrates' court, and whose cases were tried and disposed of by the magistrates (cumulative percentages)*

Period between first appearance and final disposal	Pleaded		All defendants who chose trial at a magistrates' court
	Guilty to all charges	Not guilty to some or all charges	
	cum %	cum %	cum %
Same day	61	22	57
More than 1 day to less than 2 weeks	64	30	60
2 weeks to less than 4 weeks	80	43	76
4 weeks to less than 6 weeks	88	83	87
6 weeks to less than 8 weeks	94	96	94
8 weeks to less than 10 weeks	94	100	95
10 weeks or longer	100	—	100
Number on which percentage based[1]	177 = 100%	23 = 100%	200 = 100%

Table C10 *Period between committal for sentence and date of sentence for defendants who chose to be tried at a magistrates' court, but who were sent to the Crown Court for sentence (cumulative percentages)*

Period between committal for sentence and date of sentence	All defendants sent to the Crown Court for sentence only
	cum %
Less than 2 weeks	—
2 weeks to less than 4 weeks	27
4 weeks to less than 6 weeks	81
6 weeks to less than 8 weeks	89
8 weeks to less than 10 weeks	93
10 weeks or more	100
Number on which percentage based[1]	41 = 100%

[1] Excludes those not answering.

Table C11 *Proportions of defendants agreeing/disagreeing[1] with statements expressing favourable and unfavourable attitudes towards the two court systems: those who chose trial on indictment at the Crown Court and who pleaded guilty to some or all of the charges against them[2]*

	Defendant chose venue for trial: Crown Court Disposal at: Crown Court					
	Defendant pleaded not guilty to all charges			Defendant pleaded guilty to all/some charges		
	Agree	Disagree	Base[3] = 100%	Agree	Disagree	Base[3] = 100%
	%	%		%	%	
Favourable comments. Some people have said that . . .						
they had all the opportunities they needed to say what they wanted	35	61	(114)	33	63	(51)
one always gets a fair trial	24	72	(111)	24	72	(50)
the jury paid as much attention to what they said as to what the police said	68	24	(114)	68	20	(50)
one is innocent until proved guilty	44	54	(112)	59	39	(51)
Unfavourable comments. Some people said that . . .						
the whole thing was so overwhelming that they didn't always understand what was happening	65	33	(114)	71	29	(51)
there were times when they couldn't hear what was being said	59	40	(113)	67	33	(51)
the magistrate paid more attention to what the police said than to what they said	81	9	(114)	84	14	(51)
the court didn't take sufficient notice of what made them commit the offence	59	16	(112)	80	16	(50)
the man who is well off financially gets a lighter sentence from magistrates than the poor man who commits the same offence	52	32	(114)	57	37	(51)

[1] Those defendants who said spontaneously that they neither agreed nor disagreed with the statement —recorded as neutral—have been omitted from this table, which explains why the percentages do not add to 100.
[2] In this analysis actual plea entered against the charges has been used as it is felt to have more relevance to the topic under discussion, than the plea 'intended' at the time the venue decision was made.
[3] Excludes those not answering.

Table C12 *Proportions of defendants agreeing/disagreeing[1] with statements expressing favourable and unfavourable attitudes towards the two court systems: those who chose summary trial at a magistrates' court, whose cases were disposed of by the magistrates, and who pleaded guilty to all charges against them*

| | Defendant chose venue for trial: magistrates' court Disposal at: magistrates' court | | | | | |
| | Defendant pleaded guilty to all charges | | | Defendant pleaded not guilty to all/some charges | | |
	Agree %	Disagree %	Base[2] = 100%	Agree %	Disagree %	Base[2] = 100%
Favourable comments. Some people have said that . . .						
they had all the opportunities they needed to say what they wanted	64	36	(179)	63	33	(24)
one always gets a fair trial	40	56	(177)	38	58	(24)
the jury paid as much attention to what they said as to what the police said	39	15	(172)	50	17	(24)
one is innocent until proved guilty	61	36	(177)	50	46	(24)
Unfavourable comments. Some people have said that . . .						
the whole thing was so overwhelming that they didn't always understand what was happening	59	38	(179)	50	46	(24)
there were times when they couldn't hear what was being said	55	45	(179)	38	63	(24)
the magistrate paid more attention to what the police said than to what they said	68	26	(179)	63	33	(24)
the court didn't take sufficient notice of what made them commit the offence	64	29	(178)	46	33	(24)
the man who is well-off financially gets a lighter sentence from magistrates than the poor man who commits the same offence	53	42	(179)	42	42	(24)

[1] Those defendants who said spontaneously that they neither agreed nor disagreed with the statement —recorded as neutral—have been omitted from this table, which explains why the percentages do not add to 100.

[2] Excludes those not answering.

Table C13 *Proportions of defendants who found the experience of going to court on this occasion an ordeal: those who chose the venue for their trial and those who reported having no choice of venue*

	Venue for trial					
	Crown Court		Magistrates' court			
	Disposal at		Disposal at			
	Crown Court		Magistrates' court		Crown Court	
	Going to court was an ordeal	Base[1] = 100%	Going to court was an ordeal	Base[1] = 100%	Going to court was an ordeal	Base[1] = 100%
	%		%		%	
All defendants who chose the venue for their trial	78	(161)	66	(200)	63	(43)
All defendants who reported having no choice of venue for their trial	78	(88)	41	(22)	(7)	(8)

Table C14 *Proportions of defendants who thought that magistrates should be able, in certain circumstances, to commit defendants who choose to be tried by them, to a higher court for sentence: those who chose the venue for their trial and those who reported having no choice of venue*

	Venue for trial			
	Crown Court		Magistrates' court	
	Disposal at			
	Crown Court		Magistrates' court	
	Magistrate should be able to commit	Base[1] = 100%	Magistrate should be able to commit	Base[1] = 100%
	%		%	
All defendants who chose the venue for their trial	48	(164)	44	(195)
All defendants who reported having no choice of venue for their trial	46	(92)	45	(22)

[1] Excludes those not answering.

Appendix D

The interview questionnaires

Three separate questionnaires were developed for use in this enquiry; one for those defendants whose cases had been tried and disposed of at magistrates' courts, one for defendants who had gone for trial to the Crown Court, and the third for those defendants who had been committed to the Crown Court from the magistrates' court for sentence.

The questionnaire administered to defendants whose cases had been tried and disposed of at magistrates' courts is reproduced here in full. Other questionnaires used in this enquiry are available on request from the Social Survey Division of OPCS.

IN CONFIDENCE

JAMES COMMITTEE — SURVEY OF DEFENDANTS

COURT			PERSON NO		

SERIAL NO:

INTERVIEWER   : _____

AUTHORISATION NO: _____

DATE OF INTERVIEW: _____ 1974

SEX OF INFORMANT: MALE.............1

                       FEMALE 2

PLACE OF INTERVIEW:

                  penal institution 1

                  other 2

COMPLETE A NON-RESPONSE SHEET FOR ANY DEFENDANT NOT INTERVIEWED

We are particularly interested in the experiences that people have had of two types of court; the magistrates' court, and the higher court, which is sometimes called the sessions, the assizes or the Crown Court.

1   Apart from your recent case at ....,on.............,
have you ever been to a court before ....

	No	Yes	Mag.Ct.	Higher Ct.	Other Ct.	DK
			if YES ask (a) below and code here			
INDIVIDUAL PROMPT						
(a) as a member of a jury?	1	2	3	4	5	6
(b) as a defendant, accused of an offence yourself?	1	2	3	4	5	6
(c) to bring a case against someone else?........	1	2	3	4	5	6
(d) as a witness in a case?	1	2	3	4	5	6
(e) to watch what went on?.........	1	2	3	4	5	6
(f) for any other reason?	1	2	3	4	5	6

If YES ask (a)

(a) When you went to court ....
was it to a magistrates' court, a higher court
with a judge and jury, or was it to some other kind
of court?

CODE IN GRID ABOVE
CODE ALL THAT APPLY

Can we talk now about this recent case of yours..........
Some people have said that they have been to court charged
with an offence but they have never been really sure of what
exactly they were supposed to have done.

2   First of all, can you tell me what offence(s) you think you
were charged with?

[IF INCORRECT/DON'T KNOW TELL INFORMANT
    WHAT COURT RECORDS SHOW HE WAS CHARGED WITH]

IN CONFIDENCE: CASE HISTORY to be completed BEFORE Interview

(i) Name of court: _____Magistrates' Court

(ii) Date of disposal: _____1974

OFFENCE (description)	VERDICT	SENTENCE

85

3   Your case came up at ....Magistrates' Court: when you went there for the first time did you, personally, say that you wanted this case of yours to be heard at the Magistrates' Court rather than at a higher court with a judge and jury, or did you have no say in the matter at all?

DEFENDANT CHOSE venue	1 - onto Qn. 14
No say in the matter	2

For many offences the defendant has the right to say whether he wants his case heard at the Magistrates' Court or at the Crown Court with a judge and jury.

May I just check...........

4   Do you remember the clerk at the Magistrates' Court asking you whether you wanted to have your case heard there, or whether you wanted to go to the Crown Court and be tried before a judge and jury?

Yes, remember being asked.........	1 - ask (a)
No, do not remember	2

IF YES REMEMBER BEING ASKED (1)

(a)   Did you realise at that time that the choice of where your case was to be heard was being left up to you?

Yes realised.............	4
No.....................	5

5   Could you always hear clearly what was being said to you when you were at the Magistrates' Court?

Yes..............	1
No	2

CHECK BACK TO QN. 4:

If code 1 is ringed :	DEFENDANT CHOSE venue	1 - onto Qn. 14
If code 2 is ringed :	Defendant had	
	NO CHOICE of venue	2

IMPORTANT: Remember whether DEFENDANT CHOSE venue
           OR whether defendant had NO CHOICE of venue

TO THOSE WHERE DEFENDANT HAD NO CHOICE OF VENUE FOR TRIAL

6   When you went to the magistrates' court for the first time
    for this case   , did you think that you,personally, would
    be able to say whether you wanted to have your case heard
    at the magistrates' court or at the Crown Court?

                                    Yes........................... 1
                                    No 2

7   What made you think that?

                              I was told by the police 1
                              I was told by a solicitor 2
                              From previous cases I had
               CODE ALL   appeared in as a defendant.......... 3
               THAT APPLY   From previous cases I had
                                   appeared in, not as a defendant...... 4
                              Other answers (specify)................ 5

    PROBE FULLY

8   If you had been able to decide for yourself where your case
    was to be heard, would you have asked to go to the magistrates'
    court or to the Crown Court where you could be tried before a
    judge and jury?

                                    Magistrates' Court .... 1)
                                    Crown Court .... 2) - ask (a)
                                                                         next page

87

IF MAGISTRATES' COURT (1) OR CROWN COURT (2)
(a) Why is that?

<table>
<tr><td rowspan="5">CODE ALL
THAT APPLY</td><td>Solicitor's advice) DO NOT PROBE</td><td>..................</td><td>1</td></tr>
<tr><td>Police advice) FOR ADVICE</td><td>..................</td><td>2</td></tr>
<tr><td>Better chance of being found not guilty</td><td>................</td><td>3</td></tr>
<tr><td>Better chance of getting a lighter sentence</td><td>............</td><td>4</td></tr>
<tr><td>Other answers (specify)</td><td>.................................</td><td>5</td></tr>
</table>

PROBE FULLY

[If more than one reason given read back
answer to informant and ask (i)]

only one reason given   DNA x

(i) And out of (all) these which would you say was the
main reason?

If code 1-4 above, specify code here   [ ]

Otherwise underline main reason in specified answer
above, or specify here ↓

9   You were asked in Court whether you were pleading guilty or
not guilty.
How did you plead?

Guilty to <u>all</u> charges.............	1 – ask (a)
Guilty to <u>only</u> <u>some</u> charges	2
Not guilty to <u>all</u> charges.........	3
Don't know	4

<u>IF GUILTY TO ALL CHARGES</u> (1)

(a) But if you had been <u>not guilty</u> of the offence (any of the
offences) would you have wanted to be tried at the
Magistrates' Court or at the Crown Court?

Magistrates' Court	1 – onto Qn. 30
Crown Court	2 – see instruction below

[USE CODE 3 <u>ONLY</u> AFTER REPEATING QN.   ]   But I was guilty .... | 3 – onto Qn.30

> Check back to Qn. 8
> If code 2 (Crown Court) is ringed, Qn. 9(a)(i)..... ....
> If code 1 (Magistrates' Court)is ringed
> ask ⌐

x – onto Qn.30

(i)   Why, if you had been not guilty,would you have
preferred to have been tried at the Crown Court?

Because	– there is a jury to listen to your case	1
	– you.can be represented in court by a lawyer	2
MULTI-CODE	– there is a greater chance of being acquitted...	3
	– there is a greater chance of a light sentence................................	4
	Other answers (<u>specify</u>)..........	5

– onto Qn.30

> On to Qn. 30

10 Do you think the verdict – whether you were found guilty or not
    guilty – would have been the same if you had gone to the Crown
    Court for trial?

                              Yes, same for **ALL** offences ....   1 – onto Qn. 30
                              No ....   2 – ask (a)

        IF NO(2)
        (a) Why do you think that?

                                                                    On to Qn. 30

        [Questions 11 – 13 incl. are omitted]

<u>TO THOSE WHERE</u> DEFENDANT CHOSE VENUE FOR TRIAL

14   Even <u>before</u> the clerk at the magistrates'court told you, did
      you know that you were going to be asked to say whether you
      wanted your case to be heard at the Magistrates' Court or at
      the Crown Court?

                              Yes,knew ....1 – ask (a)
                              No, did not know 2

        <u>If YES, KNEW</u> (1)
        (a) How did you know about this right to choose?
            Was it........   Yes   No

                    from previous cases you had appeared in
                      accused of doing something yourself?................. ...1........0

                    from watching the cases that appeared before
                      yours on the day you went to court for
INDIVIDUAL   this offence? ....2........0
PROMPT
                    from (any) other cases you had been to, but
                      not as a defendant?............................... ...3........0

                    from the police? ....4........0

                    from a solicitor? ....5........0

                    or in some other way? (<u>specify</u>) ....6........0

15 You chose to have your case heard at the Magistrates' Court.
    Why did you want to have your case heard there rather than
    go to the Crown Court?

                              Solicitors advice)   DO NOT PROBE   ...   1
                              Police advice   ) ─ FOR ADVICE   ...   2
                                                                   ...
                 CODE ALL   Better chance of being found
                 THAT APPLY   not guilty 3

                              Better chance of getting a
                                 lighter sentence 4

                              Other answers (specify)............. 5

PROBE FULLY

    ┌   ┐
    │ If more than one reason given read back   │
    │ answer to informant and ask (a)   │
    └   ┘

                          Only one reason given DNA . . . .| x

    (a) And out of (all) these which would you
         say was the main reason?

         If code 1-4 above, specify code here   ┌──────┐
                                                 │   │
                                                 └──────┘

         Otherwise underline main reason in specified
         answer above or specify here ┐
                                       ↓

16   Did you think that, at that time, you knew enough about
     Magistrates' Courts and Crown Courts to decide where to
     have your case heard?

                                             Yes............... | 1
                                             No .... | 2

     You were asked in court whether you were pleading guilty or
     not guilty.
17   How did you plead?

                          Guilty to all charges .... | 1 – ask (a)
                          Guilty to only some charges .... | 2
                          Not guilty to all charges .... | 3
                          Don't know .... | 4

          IF GUILTY TO ALL CHARGES (1)
          (a) But if you had been not guilty of the offence
               (any of the offences), would you still have
               wanted to be tried at the Magistrates' Court,
               or would you have chosen to go to the Crown
               Court instead?

                                  Magistrates' Court .... | 1 – onto Qn.27
                                  Crown Court .... | 2 – ask (i)
          [USE CODE 3 ONLY AFTER REPEATING   ] But I was guilty............ | 3 – Onto Qn.27
                    THE QN. | next page

          IF CROWN COURT (2)
          (i) Why, if you had been not guilty of the offence,
               (any of the offences), would you have preferred to
               have been tried at the Crown Court?

          Because – there is a jury to listen to your case........ | 1 ⎫
                   – you can be represented in court by a | ⎪
                         lawyer ....| 2 ⎬ – Onto Qn.27
          MULTI-   – there is a greater chance of being acquitted...| 3 ⎪   on next page
          CODE   – there is a greater chance of a light sentence..| 4 ⎭

                           Other answers (specify)........ | 5

18   Do you think the verdict – whether you were found
     guilty or not guilty – would have been the same if
     you had gone for trial at the Crown Court?

                          Yes, same verdict for ALL offences.... | 1
                          No .... | 2 – ask (a)
          IF NO (2)
          (a) Why do you think that?

                    (Questions 19–26 incl. are omitted)

You may have mentioned some of these points already, but may
I just check ....

At the time you had to choose where to have your case heard...

27 Did you know that if you chose to go to the Crown Court for
    trial .... ?
    [PROMPT ITEMS FROM GRID BELOW   ]

    If NO ask (a) If you had known this, do you, think you would
                 still have chosen to be tried at the Magistrates'
                 Court, or would you have asked to go to the Crown
                 Court instead?

INDIVIDUAL PROMPT:

		Yes	No	Mag.Ct.	Cr.Ct.	D.K.
A:	There would be a jury to listen to your case	1	2	4	5	6
B.	It is usual to have a qualified person, like a lawyer, in court to represent you	1	2	4	5	6
C:	There was likely to be a long wait before your case came up	1	2	4	5	6
D:	You could find out what the evidence against you was, before you even went to court	1	2	4	5	6
E:	Your case is always heard by someone who has had a lot of legal training and experience	1	2	4	5	6

If No ask Qn27(a)
code here

28 If you could have been tried at the Crown Court, without there
    being a jury, would you have wanted to have your case heard there
    or not?

                                    Yes,at Crown Court   1
                                    No.....................   2

94

29 At the time, how important was it to you, personally, that
    you had the right to choose where you wanted to have your
    case heard?   Was it ....

                                        very important............ | 1 |
                      RUNNING   important .... | 2 |
                      PROMPT   not very important .... | 3 | ⎤ - onto Qn.31
                                        or wasn't it important at all?.. | 4 | ⎦

30 You were never given the right to choose where you wanted to
    have this case of yours heard.   At that time, did this matter
    to you or not?
                                        Yes mattered .... | 1 |
                                        No did not matter .... | 2 |

    TO ALL

31 Why is that?

95

Can you now think about what might have happened if you had gone
to the Crown Court for trial.

32 How long do you think it would have been from the time you
committed the offence until your case came up at the Crown Court?

SPONTANEOUS: knew/was told date ....   x – also code
period below

Up to one month................   1
1 month less than 2 months......   2
2 months less than 4 months.....   3
4 months less than 6 months.....   4
6 months or longer.............   5

33 And do you think you would have been held in custody all that time,
or do you think you would have been released on bail?

Held in custody..........   1
Released on bail   2

[Question 34 is omitted]

96

35 (May I just check), for this particular case of yours, did the police ever tell you that you would be asked to say where you wanted to have your case heard?

Yes	1 - ask (a)(b)
No	2

IF YES (1)
(a) When did they tell you this?   Was it ....

when you were charged with the offence(s)....	1
RUNNING PROMPT after you were charged but before you went to the Magistrates' Court for the first time for this case	2
or was it only when you arrived at the Magistrates' Court	3

SPONTANEOUS ONLY: some other time(specify)	4

(b) And did the police simply tell you that you would be asked to say where you wanted to have your case heard, or did they suggest what you should do?

simply told of choice	1
suggested what to do	2 - ask (i)

IF SUGGESTED WHAT TO DO (2)
(i) What did they suggest; to have your case heard at the Magistrates' Court, or to go to the Crown Court?

Magistrates' Court	1
Crown Court	2
Other answer (specify)......	3

36   Did you talk to a solicitor about <u>where you should have your</u>
     <u>case heard?</u>

                                    Yes...................... 1
                                    No .... 2 - on to Qn.39

---

37   And did he/she suggest staying at the Magistrates' Court, or did
     he advise you to go to the Crown Court for trial?

     RECORD SPONTANEOUS COMMENTS ⌐ Magistrates' Court .... 1) - ask (a)
                                    Crown Court .... 2)
                                    Other answer (<u>specify</u>) .... 3 - on to Qn.39

     <u>IF MAGISTRATES' COURT</u> (1) <u>OR CROWN COURT</u> (2)
     (a) Did he explain to you why he thought you should
          ask to have your case heard at the (Magistrates'
          Court/Crown Court) or not?

                                    Yes .... 1 - ask (i) next
                                                                      page
                                    No .... 2 - on to Qn.39

98

IF YES (i)
(i) What reasons did he give you for recommending that you
go to the (Magistrates' Court/Crown Court)?

	Better chance of being acquitted..........	1
CODE ALL THAT APPLY	Better chance of a lighter sentence	2
	Other answers (specify)....................	3

PROBE FULLY

---

38   Do you think they were good reasons or not?

Yes, all good reasons	1
Only some good reasons	2 - ask (a)
No, none good	3
Don't know whether good or bad	4

IF ONLY SOME GOOD REASONS (2)
(a) Which did you, personally, think were not good reasons
for going to the (Magistrates' Court/Crown Court)?

39   Did anyone (else) suggest that you had your case heard at the
Magistrates' Court?

Yes................	1 – ask (a)
No	2

        IF YES (1)
        (a) Who (else) suggested staying at the Magistrates'
            Court?

	Relatives................	1
	Employer	2
MULTI	Friends...................	3
CODE	Others (specify).........	4

40   And did anyone (else) think you should go to the Crown Court
to have your case heard?

Yes................	1 – ask (a)
No	2

        IF YES (1)
        (a) Who (else) thought you should go to the Crown Court
            for your trial?

	Relatives	1
	Employer	2
MULTI	Friends	3
CODE	Others (specify)	4

41   Did you have a solicitor or a lawyer in court to represent
you?

Yes................... 1

No .... 2 - ask (a)

IF NO (2)

(a) Why was that?

Couldn't afford it 1

Didn't know it was possible...... 2

CODE ALL   No time to find one............. 3

THAT APPLY   Could manage on my own........... 4

Was pleading guilty anyway....... 5

Other answers (specify).......... 6

42   (Apart from your solicitor) did you have any witnesses or anyone
else in court to speak up for you?

Yes................ 1

No .... 2 - ask (a)

IF NO (2)

(a) Why was that?

Didn't know it was possible....... 1

CODE ALL   Could manage on my own 2

THAT APPLY   Other answer (specify)............ 3

If you go to a magistrates' court in London, you may find
either a magistrate known as a stipendiary magistrate
hearing the case on his own, or several magistrates, usually
three, hearing the case together.

43   When you went to the magistrates' court for this offence did you
appear in front of a stipendiary magistrate on his own, or were
there several magistrates sitting together?

stipendiary....................	1
several magistrates	2

44   Apart from being able to hear a case on his own, do you know of
any other differences between a stipendiary magistrate and the
magistrates who sit together?

Yes	1 – ask (a)
No	2

IF YES (1)
(a) What differences do you know of?

DO NOT PROMPT	Stipe. must be legally qualified...........	1
CODE ALL THAT	Stipes. receive a salary/wages	2
APPLY	Stipes.are full-time magistrates	3
	Other answers (specify)	4

102

45   If someone has their case heard by a magistrate, when is the
      magistrate told about the man's record (previous convictions)?

          [Hand Card A to informant]   Code below

46   And how about if they go to the Crown Court for trial, when is the
      judge told about the defendants' record?

          [Refer informant to Card A]   Code here

	Magistrate	Judge
Before he hears any evidence...............	1	1
After he has heard the evidence, but before he finds the person guilty or not guilty	2	2
Only after the person has been found guilty	3	3
Not at all	4	4
SPONTANEOUS ONLY Don't know................	5	5

          [Take back card A]

Introduce: Can we now go on to talk about
               the sorts of sentences that
               magistrates and judges can give,
               and about how your case was dealt with
               ....

47   Do you think that if a person <u>chooses</u> to be tried by a magistrate,
      he should always be sentenced by the magistrate, or do you think
      that a magistrate should sometimes be able to send the person to
      the Crown Court for sentence?

                                  Magistrate should always sentence.......... | 1
                                  Should be able to send to Crown Court...... | 2 - ask (a)

      <u>IF SHOULD BE ABLE TO SEND</u> (2)
      (a) Under what circumstances do you think a
          magistrate should be able to send a person
          to the Crown Court for sentence?

          CODE ALL   When they have a record................... | 1
          THAT APPLY   Other answers (<u>specify</u>).................... | 2

Check back to CASE HISTORY
if found GUILTY of ANY offence
ask ⌐
   ⎮
   ⎮
   ⎮   DNA: Not guilty to all
   ⎮   charges........   x - see
   ↓   instruction top
                                                                        p.23
48   Was your sentence about what you expected to get if you were
     found guilty or not?

                              Yes   1
                              No ....   2 - ask (a)
                              No idea what to expect   3

          IF NO (2)
          (a) Was it ....

          RUNNING   a heavier sentence than you expected........   5
          PROMPT   or a lighter sentence than you expected?.......   6

49   Do you think your sentence would have been any different
     if your case had been heard at the Crown Court?

                                   Yes..............   1 - ask (a)
                                   No..............   2

          IF YES (1)
          (a) Do you think it would have been........

                                   a heavier sentence   5
          RUNNING   or   a lighter sentence.............   6
          PROMPT   than you actually got?

[Questions 50 and 51 are omitted]

Check back to CASE HISTORY:

If charged with ONE offence only)
OR If ALL offences are the same   ) - Qn. 52   DNA ....   x - onto Qn. 53

If charged with DIFFERENT sorts of offences ask ──────┐
                                                      ┌─┘
                                                      ↓
52   Out of all the offences you were charged with, which one do you
     think was the most serious?

                    Specify : _____

┌──────────────────┐
│ Onto Qn. 55   │
└──────────────────┘

53   What do you think is the longest prison sentence you
      can get for ....[OWN OFFENCE   ]?

                                           specify here ──────────────►

                               YEARS | MONTHS

                           Cannot imprison, only fine......   x
                           Don't know......................   y

54   And what do you think is the heaviest fine you can get for
      ....[OWN OFFENCE   ]?

      £

                                           specify here ──────────────►   £

                           Cannot fine,only imprison.......   x
                           Don't know ....   y

      TO ALL

55   Thinking of any offence now, not just what you were charged with.....

      What do you think is the longest prison sentence that a
      magistrate can give for any one offence?

                                           YEARS | MONTHS

                               specify here ──────────────►

                           Cannot imprison, only fine   x
                           Don't know ....   y

56   And what do you think is the heaviest fine a magistrate
      can give for any one offence?

      £

                                           specify here ──────────────►   £

                           Don't know ....   y

57   Do you think that most magistrates would give about the
     same sentence for a similar offence, or do you think that
     the sentence would vary a lot depending on who heard the
     case?

                              About the same 1
                              Would vary.................... 2

58   And how about judges in the Crown Court..........
     Do you think that most judges would give about the same
     sentence for a similar offence, or do you think the sentence
     would vary a lot depending on who heard the case?

                              About the same 1
                              Would vary 2

Here are some things that other people have said about going to court. I'll read them out, then I'll ask you to tell me if you agree or disagree with what they say.

59 Some people have said that ....(INDIVIDUAL PROMPT), do you personally agree or disagree?

       If <u>AGREE</u>   :   do you agree strongly or mildly?

       If <u>DISAGREE</u> :   do you disagree strongly or disagree
                                   mildly?

[HAND CARD B TO INFORMANT]

INDIVIDUAL PROMPTS

		AGREE		DISAGREE		SPONT. ONLY:
		STRONGLY	MILDLY	STRONGLY	MILDLY	NEUTRAL
A:	The whole thing was so overwhelming that they didn't always understand what was happening	1	2	3	4	5
B:	There were times when they couldn't hear what was being said	1	2	3	4	5
C:	They had all the opportunities they needed to say what they wanted	1	2	3	4	5
D:	The magistrate paid more attention to what the police said than to what they said	1	2	3	4	5
E:	The court didn't take sufficient notice of what made them commit the offence	1	2	3	4	5
F:	One always gets a fair trial	1	2	3	4	5
G:	The man who is well off financially gets a lighter sentence from a magistrate than the poor man who commits the same offence	1	2	3	4	5
H:	The jury paid as much attention to what they said as to what the police said	1	2	3	4	5
I:	One is innocent until proved guilty	1	2	3	4	5

[Take back Card B]

For various offences, some of which are more serious than others, I'd now like to know whether you think it's important that the accused person can say whether he wants to be tried at the Magistrates' Court, or at the Crown Court.

First of all, I need to know how serious you think these various offences are.

> Hand Card C to informant.
> Individual prompt for each offence – EXCEPT defendant's own

60   Do you, personally, think this is a very serious offence
                                   a serious offence
                                   a minor offence
                           or   not really an offence at all?

     [Code in Col. A: then ask:]

61   And do you, personally, think that being able to choose where to be tried for this offence (either at the Magistrates' Court or at the Crown Court) is important or not important?

          [Code in Col. B: then onto next offence]

		DNA OWN OFF.	Col. A QN. 60 : HOW SERIOUS				Col. B QN: 61	
INDIVIDUAL PROMPT			VERY SERIOUS	SERIOUS	MINOR	NOT AN OFFENCE	IMP.	NOT IMP.
A:	Breaking into someone's house, during the daytime, while they are out, and stealing something................................	x	...1	...2	...3	...4	..6	..7
B:	Not having a television licence.................	x	...1	...2	...3	...4	..6	..7
C:	Deliberately damaging property, such as vandalism by football supporters on a train.....	x	...1	...2	...3	...4	..6	..7
D:	Shoplifting – taking something from a shop without paying for it.........................	x	...1	...2	...3	...4	..6	..7
E:	Rape...	x	...1	...2	...3	...4	..6	..7
F:	Dangerous driving [PROMPT IF NECESSARY: WITHOUT KILLING ANYONE] x			...1	...2	...3	...4	..6	..7
G:	Assaulting a policeman.........................	x	...1	...2	...3	...4	..6	..7
H:	Drinking and driving	x	...1	...2	...3	...4	..6	..7
I:	Travelling on public transport without paying...	x	...1	...2	...3	...4	..6	..7

[Take back Card C]

110

(i) HOUSEHOLD COMPOSITION AT TIME OF OFFENCE:

Introduce: E.g. Peoples' reactions to appearing in court
are often related to their family circumstances
at time, therefore ....

In GRID A give full details at the time of the offence for
(a) the informant
(b) the informant's spouse (if any)
(c) the HOH (if different from (a) and (b))

In GRID B give details of other members of the household at the time of
the offence

GRID A:

RING TO INDICATE HOH	RELATIONSHIP TO INFORMANT	AGE	SEX M F	MARITAL STATUS M S W	WORKING FT PT	NOT WORKING UNEMP. RETD. STUDT. OTHER
1	INFORMANT		1 2	3 4 5	1 2	3 4 5 6
2	Spouse DNA no spouse..x		1 2	3 4 5	1 2	3 4 5 6
3			1 2	3 4 5	1 2	3 4 5 6

GRID B:

		1 2	
		1 2	
		1 2	
		1 2	
		1 2	
		1 2	
		1 2	

(ii) AGE AT WHICH INFORMANT FINISHED FULL-TIME EDUCATION:

Still in full time education............9

Age (specify years) ———————————————→

(iii)   OCCUPATION AND INDUSTRY <u>AT TIME OF OFFENCE</u>

Details are required for (a) the informant
　　　　　　　　　　　　　 (b) the informant's spouse (if any)

If <u>either</u> informant or spouse were retired at time of offence
give details of their former occupation.
If <u>informant</u> was unemployed at time of offence give
details of last job.

INFORMANT		INFORMANT'S SPOUSE:	
At time of offence was: 　　　　working......1 　　　　retired.....2 　　　unemployed..3 DNA: stud't/other non- 　　　working......x – onto Qn. <u>Occupation</u>: (job,title, 　　　　　　grade)		At time of offence was: 　　　　working ....1 　　　　retired ......2 DNA: unemp/stud't/other 　　　　non-working....x – onto Qn. <u>Occupation</u>: (job,title, 　　　　　　grade)	
<u>Industry</u>:		<u>Industry</u>:	
<u>Self–employed or employee</u>: 　　　Self–employed....1 　　　Employee.........2		<u>Self–employed or employee</u>: 　　　Self–employed..1 　　　Employee.......2	
If manager/superintendent/ <u>self–employed</u>: DNA not manager etc......x <u>No of employees</u>: 　　None..............1 　　1–24............2 　　25 or more.....3		If manager/superintendent/ <u>self–employed</u>: DNA not manager etc.....x <u>No of employees</u>: 　　None.........1 　　1–24.........2 　　25 or more...3	

62 Now that the case is over, if you could go back and choose
    (again), would you (still) want to be tried at a Magistrates'
    Court, or would you want to go before a judge and jury at
    the Crown Court?

                                        Magistrates' Court............. 1
                                        Crown Court .... 2 - ask (a)
                                        Wouldn't matter/not bothered 3

    IF CROWN COURT (2)
    (a) Why is that?

                        CODE ALL   Would be acquitted 1
                        THAT APPLY   Would get a lighter sentence 2
                                     Other answers (specify).......... 3

63 Did you find the experience of going to court for this offence
    an ordeal, or not?

                                        Yes, ordeal .... 1 - ask (a)
                                        No 2

    IF YES, ORDEAL (1)
    (a) What do you think could have been done to
         make the whole thing less of an ordeal?

113

Check back to CASE HISTORY:

IF FOUND GUILTY OF ANY OFFENCE

Not guilty to ALL offences Qn. 64 & 65 DNA ..... x – onto Qn. 66

64   Have you put in an appeal against your conviction
      (against being found guilty)?

                                          Yes 1
                                          No 2

65   And have you appealed against your sentence?

                                          Yes 4
                                          No 5

TO ALL

66   Could I just check, have you ever been found guilty of any
      other offence, however minor?
                                          Yes .... 1 – ask (a)
                                          No 2

      IF YES (1)
      (a) Have you ever been sentenced to prison, to borstal
           training, to a detention centre or given any other
           sort of custodial sentence (before this)?

                                          Yes 3
                                          No 4

67   Finally, before I finish, is there anything else
      about this recent experience of yours in court,
      that I haven't covered, that you'd like to tell
      me about?

                                          No 1
                                          Yes (specify) 2

      ┌───┐
      │ THANK INFORMANT FOR COOPERATION   │
      │ LEAVE LEAFLET   │
      └───┘

Printed in England for Her Majesty's Stationery Office by The Campfield Press, St. Albans
(22102) Dd. 290122 K.12 3/76 Gp. 3319